Serving the Needs of Your Smart Kids

How School Leaders Create a Supportive Culture for the Advanced Learner

Brenda K. Small, Ed.D.

Gifted
UNLIMITED

Edited by: Lindsey Reinert, Ed.D.
Interior design: The Printed Page
Cover design: Kelly Crimi

Published by
Gifted Unlimited, LLC
12340 U.S. Highway 42, No. 453
Goshen, KY 40026
www.giftedunlimitedllc.com

ISBN: 978-1-953360-05-2

Acknowledgements

This book is dedicated to the students, teachers, and parents who have given me the opportunity to learn from them in how to effectively lead a school that strives to meet each of their needs.

"The great danger for most of us is not that our aim is too high and we miss it, but that it is too low and we reach it."

—Michelangelo

Preface

I believe in courage. I can see it in the people around me. In a school, I can see it in my students, their teachers, other administrators and parents. It is obvious when it is not present. It takes courage to *effectively* lead a school. It takes courage to *effectively* raise a child.

As a principal of several schools with high achieving students, I noticed the barriers to their learning soon after I started the job. They were easy to see. They were in front of me and amplified when a staff member or even my supervisor drew a line in the sand and said "no, we cannot do that." Do not stand in the way of student learning on my watch.

As I started outlining the content of this book, it occurred to me that every school principal should be automatically taking these actions. Is a book needed to tell them how to meet the needs of high achieving students? I have taught education leadership courses at the masters and doctoral level for over 10 years in 4 different universities. We don't cover this. That's right, Gifted Education was not in any syllabi.

I am a believer in our education system. This equity of education is one of our last chances to reach out to the underserved student and their families. The research is out there. We are missing the gifted identification of our underserved students. They are in our nation's classrooms waiting for their teachers and leaders to have the courage to notice them and meet their high achieving needs. We (all educators) have the opportunity to change their legacy and those of their future children. Oh, the power of meeting a student's needs! Look into their eyes and find an answer for them.

School leaders are retiring or leaving the profession and fewer candidates are available to replace them in our nation's schools. Superintendents are claiming the incoming leaders have less teaching and administrative experience. This is difficult work. Now more than ever, it is critical that we support school leaders through mentoring and publications like this book. All school leaders are called to find their focus and passionately pursue it. Be committed to keep the student at the center of your decisions. This commitment takes perseverance and courage to boldly break down barriers for your students and their families.

Read the three parts of this book as a school leader, teacher, gifted advocate, parent, aunt or friend. I believe "we get what we work for." Leaders, work for a shift in meeting the needs of high-achieving students in every school in our nation. Parents, work toward acquiring the knowledge needed to be empowered in your child's education. Make this book the first step in your journey.

The student-centered school starts with the courage of a student-centered leader.

Contents

Part One

Why School Leaders Must Be Active in Meeting the Needs of All Advanced Learners

I will not follow where the path may lead,
but I will go where there is no path,
and I will leave a trail.

—Muriel Strode
American Poet & Author, 1875-1930

Introduction to Part One

These chapters in *Part One* provide a foundation for the leadership and laws governing gifted education. The reader is introduced to the journey of advocating for our advanced learners. It takes more than knowledge to make these changes. It takes a type of leadership that moves barriers. These barriers are wide and vast between the status quo of serving high achievers in today's schools and taking action to do what is right to nurture these young brilliant minds.

The identity of a school leader is found in their priorities in the school they lead. Look down the halls. Ask students to define their school administration. Ask teachers to give pluses and deltas about their supervisors. What will the answers reveal? The priorities of the leadership will be exposed. Is serving all students a priority? Where are the gifted students in the leader's priorities?

The multiple definitions of the gifted child and the laws governing their support are provided to the reader. Take this information and use it as a foundation of facts to assist in an advocacy plan for high achievers. Use the detailed definitions, characteristics and even the laws to support a cause for change.

A caution to the parents and other advocates of gifted children. This section provides information on the definition of "gifted" and the lengthy historical legislation attempting to support their unique learning needs. Although important, this foundational information may not be as interesting to a parent as *Part Three.*

Parents of high achievers experience daily challenges in their quest to support these young minds. Be aware that school leaders see the parents' journeys from an experienced, yet peripheral lens.

A visionary leader actively seeks out the needs of all the learners in their school. Parents are called to use their voices. As a parent on a school leader selection committee, pursue this visionary style. Parents are the school leader's partner in creating a nurturing pathway to graduation. Furthermore, as a parent researching the best school for their gifted child, pursue a school whose leader places a priority on actively supporting all levels of learners.

CHAPTER 1
To School Leaders:
Is your priority to serve all students?

Gifted students sit in classrooms across the world. Some of these students are fully identified and recognized for their talents. They enjoy the proper support and resources from their education system. Others may have the paperwork to indicate their giftedness, but their learning environment does not differentiate from the rest of the student body. And even more critical, is the presence of gifted students who are not identified due to the barriers fabricated by schools or the school districts through their policies and procedures. The EdWeek Research Center reported in a Gifted Education national survey that an average 12 percent of students are defined as gifted, respondents say. Among students identified as gifted, 68 percent are receiving services.[1]

According to the National Association of Gifted Children[2] between 10 and 15 percent of students in an average school are gifted students. Yet, the U.S. Department of Education's Office of Civil Rights[3] estimates that only six percent of public school students are enrolled in gifted and talented programs. This percentage occurs regardless of the location, rate of poverty, minority ratios, etc. Are all of these students receiving the resources needed to excel at the top of their ability level? Can educators identify the gifted students in their school? Or are these unidentified gifted students labeled as behavior problems which results in teachers who may be unwilling to acknowledge their active mind is disengaged. Why are these students not provided with the fuel needed to excel toward their full potential?

Gifted students are one of our world's most valuable natural resources and their future is in the hands of our educational leaders. These leaders have a responsibility to know what is needed to enhance their education. There are gifted adults who look back at their Kindergarten through 12th grade experience and indicate that they "have been robbed" of their learning at their full potential. In their adult life, they learned about their gifts and "how to learn" more efficiently and effectively. These conditions exist, yet, school leaders profess to "do no harm" to the children in their care.

As an academic leader, how is your school serving the gifted learner? It is understood, and required, that there are strategies in place for raising the lowest learners to grade level. Look around, what are the strategies for the high achievers? These pages outline such strategies. Start the innovative action plan with the mindset the leader is responsible in serving the low and the high learners.

To start, ask why you chose to be a headmaster, principal or director. This reflection most likely includes the promise to enhance the learning of all children. Look down the halls of a school. Notice that all children are diverse in their looks, actions, and learning capabilities. So, what does it mean to create a learning environment for all children? School leaders have a special power in their school: resource control.

Now, as a school leader, ask yourself your honest opinion of the gifted student. Not the professional opinion; what is your personal opinion? An image of one of your gifted students will come to mind. Think about that student's environment. Is it the most effective environment to nurture the student's academic and social growth? It is assumed that each school leader ensures the state and federal mandates are carried out as required.

Are these mandates followed as a "check off" and not constantly evaluated for effectiveness?

Visualize the gifted student again.
Are these "checked off" mandates all they need?
No, probably not.
Stir up the resources and be ready to impact student learning.

The basic needs of an advanced learner are simple to explain

Think of your students as a car with an engine. The lower achiever is given fuel, a pit crew of support, and even a push to drive toward her greatest potential in school. The pit crew is alert and ready to intervene if there is even the slightest sign of struggle or if an essential part of the support system breaks down. The regular student learning "at grade level" drives with the group and everyone is receiving similar amounts of fuel and support as their learning peers. They stay nose to nose with the others most of the time. Occasionally they will accelerate or drop behind depending on the road conditions (teacher, home life, etc.).

The advanced learner's engine is revving when driven in tandem with the "at grade level" students. Only the minimum amount of fuel and support are provided to stay with the pack. Yet, the revving engine is noticed by the other cars and their leaders. It wants to go faster. The revving and frustration are mimicking "The Little Engine That Could" saying: "I think I can, I think I can." These cars require a high-octane fuel, unique support and even perhaps a different road to safely excel to their full potential. Being relegated to drive next to the other cars gives the driver two choices. The first is to use her frustration to create chaos and goof off. The second choice is to let off of the accelerator and stay with the pack, never experiencing her true potential.

The choice on how fast the car can go is dependent on the distribution of resources. It may be assumed the educator has adequate knowledge of the research needed to support each level of learner. From the lower level learner to the advanced learner, the resources and information reside within the leader's reach.

Now, take a moment to observe two different leadership styles

A school leadership style can encompass the responsibility of completing tasks that meet established goals. Or, a school leadership style can have the self-assigned responsibility of taking on a student centric servant-leader mindset. Can highly effective school leaders embody both types of leadership?

Task Centric Leaders

On one hand, there is a leader who is *task centric*. The daily responsibilities, including a set schedule, routine meetings, and closely monitored paperwork are followed with predictable expectations from support staff and students. Innovation is observed through a safe, predictable plan of action with a clear hesitation to upset the status quo which is working fine...thank you.

Visionary Servant Leaders

On the other hand, there is the *servant leader*. This leader notices the ever-changing affective environment of the staff, students and parents. Innovation strategies and new information on student needs are readily accepted as a challenge to meet successfully.[4] When a stressor occurs, this leader responds to the people's needs as a priority. The managerial tasks and required paperwork are frequently delegated to highly effective *task centric* subordinates.

The visionary servant school leader is attentive to their school's ever-changing needs. The environment shifts each school year with the arrival of the new class of students. The gifted learner's need for support is on this leader's radar. Using collaborative leadership and innovative strategies, these leaders effectively respond to the needs of each of their students, staff and parents.

Let's look at the tasks of the day. The visible leadership is in place: first to arrive at school in the morning, classroom walkthroughs are complete, frequent cafeteria appearances, bus ramp visits before and after school, attendance at evening events, etc. The managerial leadership tasks are in place: completed reports to the district office, staff positions filled, evaluations complete, facilities repaired, budgets balance, parent meetings scheduled, and email is down to a tolerable level. The school leader is carrying out what is expected by raising or maintaining student test scores, increasing graduation rates, managing student discipline, and keeping complaints out of the front office. Ultimately the school leader will face a crossroads in meeting the needs of all students in the school.

The school's "book cover" looks great. Turn to the pages on the inside and they will reveal if the school leader is serving all the levels of student learners. The *task centric* leader will admire the cover proudly. The *servant leader* will open the book to dig deeper into how to serve all student learners. The gifted student is on the inside waiting and wanting to receive the attention of the school's staff so she can excel above everyone's expectations.

Why focus on leadership style?

This reflection will give the leader the "why" for their actions in making changes or not making changes for their students. Let's face it, the paycheck of administrators stays the same with or without positive changes for their gifted students. Of course, a drop-in reading and math scores or graduation rates will earn an inquiring eye from the school district and even the state department of education. Consequently, more resources will follow the downturn in the lower level students' learning decline.

Yet, the gifted students are not on this radar. They are moving through the system like water down a stream silently avoiding barriers and gaining ground through time spent self-navigating the processes. Does this mean they are prepared to enter the next grade level at the top of their abilities? Or, are these gifted students simply good at navigating the school environment with a "go along to get along" mindset?

This is where the student's future is in the hands of the school leader. This visionary leader recognizes there are vast natural resources to be tapped within their school. Moving away the compliance curtain put up by so many of the gifted students, will reveal much work to accomplish to serve these underserved children.

It takes work to discover the advanced student gaps within a school's infrastructure. It takes even more work to displace current thoughts and practices to create a stimulating, nurturing and productive environment. This purposeful action is critical in the leader's quest to serve the high achieving student at their ability level.

As school leaders shift their school infrastructure into enhancing the advanced student environment, a light will shine on the overall accomplishments of the school. It is this population of students who can and will bring up the student academic learning at all levels. A tidal wave of accelerated and blended classes, additional extra-curricular offerings, poignant teacher training and relevant social and emotional resources will hit all levels of learners with new opportunities to excel.

What is inside this book for the school leader, parents of gifted children and the community supporting gifted education?

This book will give readers practical tools to enhance the learning environment of their gifted students at any age from grades kindergarten through their senior year of high school. We start with the school leader's power to change the school's infrastructure.

These opportunities reside within the walls of every educational institution. A light illuminates the problems and a plethora of solutions. The costs and other resources are considered with each initiative.

The focus remains on *what is best for the student* with all conversations, initiatives and ideas.

Yet, it is the ***school leader's*** choice to move from the task manager to the visionary leader. The enlightened leader who uses the practical applications within these pages will see all levels of learners in the school excel beyond past expectations. The ripple of this positive leadership throughout the school will be noticed by the students, teachers, parents, community, and district supervisors. It is exciting to witness the positive stories coming out of schools after a visionary school leader takes these steps to serve their underserved gifted student population.

The ***parents*** of the gifted student are provided with strategies in this book which are applicable to the nation's learning institutions. Authority structures in schools are called upon to inspire the confidence of parents. This trust encourages parents to know their children are safe and learning what is appropriate through state requirements.

"The first step to providing an improved accelerated education plan is to learn additional facts about the needs of their own gifted student" according to the Colorado Department of Education.[5] Parents have the power to enhance their child's learning through a few simple actions. The information in this book will explain how a variety of organizational structures can provide opportunities to successfully carry out these actions.

Experienced ***school leaders and parents*** of gifted students will recognize the children in the scenario insets within this book. Each scenario is written from a true-life experience with a gifted student. As with most education books, the objective is to enhance the learning of students. These gifted children scenarios provide a reality in the practical application of the tools. They are at the center of each suggestion.

Reading Discussion Activities

1. In 3 or more well-constructed sentences, write your personal mission. These sentences reveal your reason for becoming (or preparing to become) a school leader.
2. Describe your leadership style in detail using the terminology from this chapter. Explain why you are one of the 2 leadership styles described. Give 3 specific experiences as examples to illustrate your claim.
3. Explain your current perception of the characteristics and needs of a student identified as gifted.

Chapter 2
As a School Leader, Can You Describe the Gifted Student?

What is the difference between a highly motivated student and a gifted student? This difficult question can be answered by looking at the opposite situation. There are students identified as gifted who do not excel in their schoolwork. Their teachers will question the test results of an underachieving gifted student because of their low grades and lack of motivation to participate in class. Yet, other students not identified as gifted are highly motivated to complete homework, participate in class and have good test scores. Consequently, the various definitions of the Gifted Student are important, yet somewhat varied as articulated by academic researchers.

The gifted student is changing as our world population transforms. Educators are asked to evolve into a mindset where they notice the accelerating student is arriving from more diverse populations. Recognition of student potential and the appreciation of the abilities of all students is essential.

This inclusive view brings a welcome lens into our schools as children with diverse linguistic, cultural and educational backgrounds enrich our school environments. The utilization of objective measurements of a student's abilities that is not dependent on verbal acuity, but is dependent on the thinking processes, is critical for the increasingly diverse classroom.

Following are several definitions of what it means to be gifted from credible sources in gifted research:

The National Association for Gifted Children (NAGC) provides a definition that reflects higher-level thinking skills and a multi-faceted need for support services.

"Gifted individuals are those who demonstrate outstanding levels of aptitude (defined as an exceptional ability to reason and learn) or competence (documented performance or achievement in top 10% or rarer) in one or more domains. Domains include any structured area of activity with its own symbol system (e.g., mathematics, music, language) and/or set of sensorimotor skills (e.g., painting, dance, sports)."[1]

The Columbus Group developed this definition in 1991 that is utilized by researchers and professionals to differentiate the gifted mind from the norm.

"Giftedness is asynchronous development in which advanced cognitive abilities and heightened intensity combine to create inner experiences and awareness that are qualitatively different from the norm. This asynchrony increases with higher intellectual capacity. The uniqueness of the gifted renders them particularly vulnerable and requires modifications in parenting, teaching and counseling in order for them to develop optimally."[2]

The Jacob Javits Gifted and Talented Students Education Act from the Elementary and Secondary Education Act written to increase the bodies of gifted research defines gifted students as:

"Students, children, or youth who give evidence of high achievement capability in areas such as intellectual, creative, artistic, or leadership capacity, or in specific academic fields, and who need services and activities not ordinarily provided by the school in order to fully develop those capabilities."[3]

The federal definition of Gifted and Talented is utilized for funding and research.

"The term 'gifted and talented,' when used with respect to students, children, or youth, means students, children, or youth who give evidence of high achievement capability in such areas as intellectual, creative, artistic, or leadership capacity, or in specific academic fields, and who need services or activities not ordinarily provided by the school in order to fully develop those capabilities."[4]

State definitions of the Gifted and Talented vary in content and requirement of what is needed in the classroom to serve the student. Many provide definitions that compare students of the same age. Several states do not require schools to follow the state definition. Additionally, states may not differentiate between levels of giftedness. For example, scores between 130 and 140 on an IQ test require different services from the child who scores between 150 and 180. Review the Commission of Education for the United States to determine the state definition.[5]

The definition of gifted is varied. The advanced learner who is not identified as gifted may possess many of the same characteristics and needs. This resource provides information, guidance and encouragement in the serving of all high achievers regardless of their identification.

The characteristics of gifted students in every school

The characteristics of the gifted student are vast and encompass unique variables. Experienced teachers reveal that they know a gifted student after they have spent just a few class periods with them. Many schools depend on the teacher to recommend a student be tested for gifted identification. For teachers at all grade levels, training on accurately making these judgments is beneficial.

Below are a few outlining characteristics of gifted students compiled from the author's experiences and The National Association for Gifted Children's sources:

Gifted Characteristics[6]

Academically Minded	**Behavioral**
Curiosity is prevalent in most situations	Observant of their environment regardless of the subject or content
Constantly trying alternative solutions from the status quo	Ability to concentrate for longer periods than their peers
Fast thinkers, quick processers	Displays high expectations of their personal abilities and those of others
Maintains a deep understanding of a variety of subjects	Memory is advanced
Catches onto new concepts quickly	Shows innovative concepts and creative initiative in multiple areas
Knowledge of extended vocabulary	Ability to consistently multi-task
Recognizes complex relationships and patterns	Shows interest in diverse activities
Keen power of abstraction	Self-acceptance and unconcern for social norms
Interest in problem-solving and applying concepts	Intensely focused on passions
Persistent, goal directed behavior	Volatile temper, especially related to perceptions of failure
Independence in work and study	Constantly questions
Voracious and early reader	Boundless enthusiasm
Idealism and a high sense of justice	Highly energetic, needs little sleep or downtime
Diversity of interests and abilities	Impulsive, eager and spirited
Power of critical thinking, skepticism and self-criticism	Perseverance, strong determination in areas of importance

Clark, B. (2008). *Growing up gifted (7th ed.)* Upper Saddle River, NJ: Pearson Prentice Hall.

The unique needs of gifted students defined through the lens of a school leader

School leaders do not always have the training or a keen eye for recognizing a student as gifted or the insight to determine if a gifted student is struggling. A simple curiosity and observant interest in students start the inquiry into their abilities and, perhaps, even lead to a recommendation for testing or the application of additional resources. Such informed observations open doors for students. The power of the school leader starts with a willingness to observe and ask questions of the student, teachers and their parents.

Take a look at two scenarios of high achieving learners: James and Sarah.

The story of James:

James is one of 24 seventh graders sitting in a required World Cultural Geography class. He is identified as Gifted with a 130 IQ. This social studies class has a difficult group of students who have chronic behavior issues addressed daily by their frustrated teacher.

His school provides gifted services in his English class. He is one of the pack in his other classes. James has calculated the percentage values of all of his assignments in each class. He knows he does not have to complete his homework or the worksheets to receive an "A" for each class. In English, the teacher provides additional assignments for those students identified as gifted. He is one of the top students in each class, but he is bored in his classes. His teachers allow him to read his robotics books while they teach. They all love having him in class and his principal knows he is the top in their chess team. James amuses himself at home by taking free online classes in robotics from a national university. He chats with comrades online about building advanced computers.

School leaders enjoy having a "James" in their school. He will receive the highest score possible on the state accountability tests.

His near perfect attendance comes with no discipline issues and rare parent telephone calls. James will enter high school with a top-grade point average and register for a hodge podge of elective classes. His biggest decision is whether to take an average class for an "easy A" or take a more challenging course that requires homework.

Since James is identified as *gifted*, his counselor advises him to take a more rigorous schedule. Nah, he is going to take regular classes that give him free time to pursue his computer hobby. As he leaves the counselor's office with his freshman schedule, she predicts he will be one student out of her 500+ alphabetically assigned high schoolers who she will not see again until he needs college recommendation letters. He graduates in 4 years with a 4.0.

Has James's school provided him with what he needs to excel in his future?

The school leader carried out the minimum responsibility to James. The student was provided with a safe and orderly educational environment. The credits to graduate were offered efficiently at each grade level.

Answer these questions as a school leader, parent of a gifted student, and a community member:

1. Is James challenged to work at his highest potential in his school? Why or why not?
2. What actions could a school leader take to increase the learning power of James while in middle school?
3. What conversation could have taken place in his freshman counselor's office?
4. What are the initiatives the school's leader can put in place to serve James?
5. How would his adult life be different with these initiatives in place to challenge and promote a higher level of learning in his school experience prior to graduation?

The Myth: "Gifted Students don't need help; they'll do fine on their own"

Would you send a star athlete to train for the Olympics without a coach? Gifted students need guidance from well-trained teachers who challenge and support them to fully develop their abilities. Many gifted students may be so far ahead of their same-age peers that they know more than half of the grade-level curriculum before the school year begins. Their resulting boredom and frustration can lead to low achievement, despondency, or unhealthy work habits. The role of the teacher is crucial for spotting and nurturing these talents in school.[7]

The story of Sarah:

Sarah is in 2nd grade with Ms. Snell, who had her older sister, Isabella, in her class two years prior. Isabella was a less than stellar student with a below average reading level and a desire to stand and walk in the classroom at all times. Isabella eventually repeated 3rd grade and is now receiving specialized services in her second attempt. Contrarily, Sarah is quiet, does her work and socializes readily with her friends. Teachers are asked to recommend students to be tested for the Gifted and Talented Program in the fall of 2nd grade. Ms. Snell will express that she considers all her students equally for this assessment. She weighs all the variables on the check off sheet which measures a student's potential for gifted. Sarah's family background is an overriding factor for Ms. Snell. She believes Sarah is thriving in this regular school environment and by challenging her in the gifted program, she may experience unwanted behaviors similar to her sister. Sarah is denied access to the assessment which, per district policy, is only given in the second grade. Sarah will not be tested again without a champion from one of her future classrooms or schools. Ms. Snell recommends 10% of her 2nd grade class be tested for gifted.

Sarah continues her school years making passing grades in her regular courses. She quickly learns that the extra effort to earn A's has few rewards. She aligns with friends who are not high achievers. This suits her because being smart and liking school is not a popular trait in her circle of friends. Sarah will drop in academic ability by the end of elementary school. She enters middle school as an average learner, not noticed by her teachers as having gifted potential. Her boredom manifests itself into poor attendance and dropping out of high school at 16 years old.

As a school leader, how can you influence Sarah's future?

Teacher training is a crucial resource distributed by the school leader. The capacity for a teacher to recommend a student for gifted testing lies in their personal experiences, judgements, and high-quality training. Unidentified high achieving students are frequently labeled as behavior problems due to their disengaging frustration. Trained teachers have the power to combat these situations by overcoming stereotypes. They are on the front line. They are the school leaders' eyes in the classrooms.

Answer these questions as a school leader, parent of a gifted student, and a community member:

1. How can a school leader find the "Sarahs" in their school in time to serve their giftedness?

2. Does the school leader have a high expectation of teachers to accurately identify students who should be tested for gifted with the same intensity as those tested for remedial support?

3. What is the culture of the school? Does the school leader consistently refer to her embedded message that everyone who works with the children has the responsibility to notice their differences?

4. Does your school offer high quality and relevant professional development opportunities for all teachers, administrators and support staff?

5. How would Sarah's adult life be different with these initiatives in place to challenge and promote a higher level of learning in her early school experience?

The Myth: Teachers challenge all students, so gifted kids are fine in the regular classroom.

Although teachers try to challenge all students, they are frequently unfamiliar with the needs of gifted children and do not know how to best serve them in the classroom. A national study conducted by the Fordham Institute found that 58% of teachers have received no professional development focused on teaching academically advanced students in the past few years and 73% of teachers agree that "too often, the brightest students are bored and underchallenged in school —we're not giving them a sufficient chance to thrive. This report confirms what many families have known: not all teachers are able to recognize and support gifted learners".[8]

A quick overview of the academic needs of a high level learner

With the school leader's working knowledge of a *giftedness* definition, gifted characteristics, and two student scenarios, now, what is unique about their academic needs? School leaders and gifted advocates need brief talking points to express the academic needs of the gifted student. Below are four items which express these needs as simple academic identifiers of gifted children.

1. **Intellectual Peers:** Gifted students need access to their intellectual equals. These peers provide a challenge, entice stimulating discussions and enrich their individualized learning process and outcomes. A gifted comrade will propel the gifted student forward in intellectual pursuits. There is no need to re-explain or simplify a concept or explanation. Socialization builds critical social skills needed for the gifted student to experiment with group skills and teamwork.

2. **An Understanding of the Gifted Mind:** Additional classwork or homework does not meet the academic needs of gifted students. They need to be encouraged to dig deeper into the meaning of a current assignment. Their math problems need to be project-based with their intellect and problem-solving skills determining the route to the solution. Yes, this may be

more work for their teachers. They need well-trained teachers who recognize their giftedness and create specific assignments that meet their intellectual needs.

3. **Academically Appropriate Challenges:** The gifted identification does not encompass universal skills and knowledge. A student who excels in math may be a poor writer. The teacher, parent and administrator must recognize a child's strengths and weaknesses and align their expectations with that knowledge. A child who has an extensive knowledge of Shakespeare and can articulate beyond his years about the symbolism in each play, may struggle in his biology course. Forcing students to work above their level of understanding creates frustration for the student and his parents.
4. **Individualized Education:** There is a uniqueness in meeting the needs of gifted children. Their academic and social needs must be addressed as related to their individual requirements. They thrive when given individualized accelerated assignments. Additional assignments of the same learning level of their non-gifted peers is not meeting their acceleration needs. Providing students with the freedom to dig deeper into a subject they enjoy will produce the desired learning environment. The more individualized the education of the gifted students, the more they will soar toward their potential.

An abbreviated look at the social & emotional needs of the advanced learner

There is more to gifted students' minds than their intellectual abilities. There is a social and emotional need that occurs more frequently than with non-gifted peers. Those closest to our gifted children will agree that these needs may override the intellectual needs. Understanding and meeting these needs removes barriers for our gifted students.

- **The Imposter Syndrome:** This occurs when gifted students feel they are not as smart as the people around them believe they are. This syndrome is a result of the pressure from everyone around the gifted student: peers, parents, teachers, etc. Gifted students may feel like a fraud and that they do not deserve such praise and recognition. Their natural high intellectual abilities may be suppressed to avoid being noticed.[9]

- **Challenges appear in the college years:** Gifted students are conditioned to believe being smart makes everything easy. Learning *how* to learn is the first step for the gifted student to excel at a university. As academic expectations increase, the ability to adapt by knowing *how to learn* difficult academic content, enhances the student's academic and professional future.

- **I am not good at everything:** Gifted students are learning above their grade level in at least one subject. The gifted description is asynchrony, or simply, developing out of sync. "The development tends to be uneven, and they often feel out-of-sync with age peers and with age-based school expectations."[10] Students may even fall behind their peers or experience slower development in their non-gifted subjects. Students like the super-hero analogy to describe themselves: The Flash may be fast, but that does not mean he is equally as strong. Or smart. Or able to read minds. Our gifted children are superheroes.

- **Surprisingly intense at times:** Gifted students frequently exhibit other intensities or overexcitabilities. Famous Polish psychologist Kazimierz Dabrowski identified five areas of intense behaviors as psychomotor, sensual, emotional, intellectual, and imaginational with at least one being dominant.[11]

- **Do not listen to gifted stereotypes:** The gifted student has the ability to morph into the landscape or come screaming into a room. There is no accurate stereotype of a gifted child. They are as diverse as any group of children in school. The preconceptions of their identity are often used by them to avoid or attract attention.

- **Having friends is a requirement to excel:** Students need to be with their own people. The gifted student thrives with gifted peers of all ages. These stimulating conversations enhance their learning environment and increase their problem-solving abilities. Social isolation is detrimental to the gifted student's psyche.

- **Anxiety specific to the Gifted learner:** The advanced learner may be functioning at higher intellectual, emotional or imaginational rate than their peers. Just the fact that they feel different, may induce anxiety. Fitting in, making friends and trying to be "normal" can lead to anxiety and depression.[12]
- **Aversion to risk taking:** The advanced learner is accustomed to achieving at a higher level. Faced with a challenging situation, their resiliency in actually failing at something and recovering may be difficult. They tend to avoid these academic, social or physical risks which are outside their past experiences.[13]
- **The individual identity tied to the Gifted label:** When a child is recognized as gifted, resolving the feeling of being different can be an issue. Furthermore, expectations excel which adds to the new identity and may compromise the social-emotional feelings of well-being.[14]

(Adapted from CC-BY-SA, Byrdseed, LLC. and cited sources.[15]*)*

Reading Discussion Activities

1. Using the information in this chapter and personal experiences, write your own definition of a gifted student.
2. List specific action steps for creating a school policy and infrastructure change for James. Make a separate list for Sarah's needs. Include the names of staff members and dates for implementation.
3. Discuss specific students you know who have experienced one of the 6 descriptions of social and emotional needs listed. List the specific actions are needed to meet the student needs? How can you create a school support system built to recognize and address these needs?

Chapter 3
Education History and Current Laws:
A Telling Journey of Gifted Education

A study of the history of education in the United States reveals an interesting quest to serve all students. We start with the nation's founders incorporating compulsory education into the state laws. Massachusetts was the first U.S. state to enact the Compulsory Education Law of 1852.

Towns were required to offer primary schools focused on grammar and arithmetic. The objective of the law was to create a stronger union through literacy and to assimilate immigrant children. Furthermore, in the late 1800's and early 1900's compulsory education discouraged factory owners from exploiting children for child labor.[1]

An organically structured system of differentiated learning emerged with the requirement to attend school until the age of 16 in most states. Frequently, there was only one teacher who taught all students in the same "one-room schoolhouse." These early American students learned at their individual paces. A child's learning level was not determined by age, but by skill. Home tutoring of high achieving students from mostly affluent families was another standard practice of the times. These students, mostly males, found themselves entering universities at an early age.

As progress hit our nation and schools grew, students were no longer learning at their own pace with teachers who knew their individual abilities. The new collective and standardized school systems divided students by age and into individual classrooms. Motivation and academic ability were not a consideration in this model. Individualized education was no longer a value or necessity in meeting the compulsory laws. This industrial model of organization still exists in today's schools.

Advanced students were served through enriched afterschool programs and many graduated early. Yet, differentiation within the classroom was near non-existent. The second world war years brought increased motivation by universities for students to enter their programs at an early age prior to joining the armed forces.

The Ford Foundation initiated the Fund for Advanced Education in the 1950s for students by establishing the College Board Advanced Placement Program. These secondary classes held the weight of college credit. Advanced students were given the opportunity to earn college credit while attending free public schools.[2]

These Advanced Placement courses are just one of the accelerated options for our high achiever in today's secondary schools. A plethora of advanced options are available to elementary schools. However, availability of any accelerated options is dependent on the state, school district, school leader and their qualified teachers.

It was not until the watershed report, "A Nation Deceived" was released in 2004 that attention was given to the education of high achievers. This report highlighted the disparities between the research on how the gifted student learns and the actual practices in the nation's schools. The title is accurate in relating the passion and accuracy of how our schools were touting their quality acceleration programs yet missing the mark on how to excel our high achievers.[3]

The ten-year follow-up to the Nation Deceived Report was A Nation Empowered.[4] The objective of this report was to inform educators, parents, and policy makers of current research on acceleration, how that information has been applied to educational policy throughout the nation. It explains in detail how educators can use the findings to make decisions for their brightest students. The economically sound, high impact interventions are essential to the common objective of challenging and engaging the advanced learner. These two reports have impacted acceleration programming nationally.

The long and winding road to legislating support for Gifted and Talented Education

Education policy has been influenced by the federal government for most of the last century. Advocates for the inclusion of support for the Gifted and Talented students are diligently working toward increasing the legislation directly serving these important students.

Below are relevant historical legislative acts bringing change in the past 70 years. As each item is reviewed consider the level of importance placed on serving gifted students.

Historical Legislative Events in Gifted Education	
National Science Foundation Act of 1950	The National Science Foundation (NSF) was created to provide federal support for research and for the education of students in the sciences and mathematics. The supporters saw the need for resources to be provided to the brightest students to ensure the enhancement of knowledge to stay competitive in a global society.[5]
National Defense Education Act of 1958	Sputnik was launched in Russia and the U.S. reacted by passing the NDEA which provided funding to identify gifted students in science, math and world languages. School counselors were employed and trained through the NDEA which was not funded after two years.[6]
Elementary and Secondary Education Act of 1965	The (ESEA) funding has been a vehicle for establishing good education practices in the states that adopt these federal policies in exchange for funding. The ESSA experiences reauthorization every five years. Gifted and Talented inclusions have been sparse.[7]
Task Force on Gifted Persons of 1968	President Lyndon B. Johnson's task force was charged with determining how to identify the nation's brightest citizens. Their recommendations were to create a center and advisory council for the Development of Exceptionally Talented Persons. Our nation's talent search organizations remain active as a result of this Act.[8]

Marland Report of 1972	US Commissioner of Education Sidney P. Marland set a precedent by asking for individualized services for each gifted child. The amendments to the ESEA report in 1974 utilized Marland's recommendations to create the Office of Gifted and Talented in the Department of Education while providing annual federal appropriations for gifted programming. The first definition of giftedness was established through his report.[9]
Education of All Handicapped Children Act of 1975	This education act is the foundation for serving special education students. FAPE (free and appropriate public education) established benchmark legislation to which all future acts are compared. Under FAPE, all students were ensured due process rights and individual education plans (IEPs) in the least restrictive environment.
Gifted and Talented Children's Education Act of 1978	This Act provided a category for gifted and talented students within the Title IX part of ESEA and authorized increased appropriations. It slightly altered the definition of gifted by referencing children in three development stages (preschool, elementary and secondary), voiding a mention of psychomotor abilities, and confirming the need for gifted special services. The Act was repealed after President Regan signed the Omnibus Budget Reconciliation Act of 1981 which closed the Office of Gifted and Talented along with 29 other education programs.[10, 11]
Jacob K. Javits Gifted and Talented Students Education Act of 1988 National Excellence: A Case for Developing America's Talent 1993	Senator Jacob Javits of New York created this education act which reestablished the Office of Gifted and Talented as well as a National Research Center which provides resources for educators. $12 million was granted in 2017.[12]

No Child Left Behind Act, 2001	Under this education act, state funding allocations were dependent on data systems that articulated the grade level and learning level. All students were required to be at their grade learning level by 2014. Funds were diverted into the lowest quartile of learners as accountability structures, such as high stakes testing, were put in place for districts, schools and teachers.[13]
Individuals with Disabilities Education Improvement Act of 2004	After waiting seven years for an update and reauthorization, the key component affecting gifted students is the elimination of the requirement for an aptitude test to identify students. Instead a Response to Intervention (RtI) approach involving multiple student measurements is preferred.[14]
Every Student Succeeds Act of 2015	This is the reauthorization of the Elementary and Secondary Education Act of 1965 (formally NCLB). The gifted and talented are addressed through: Title I and Title II changes, state and district report cards, and approval for adaptable computer software assessments.[15]
Title I	ESSA established funds through Title 1 that may be used to identify gifted students' poverty level, provide resources, hire gifted education specialists and purchase assessments designed for English language learners.[16]
Title II	ESSA established funds for grant applications that provide training for teachers and other school staff in the identification and instructional support of gifted learners.[17]

Adapted in part from: Kristen R. Stephens, Applicable Federal and State Policy, Law, and Legal Considerations in Gifted Education, 2018.

What is the state law governing gifted education in your school? Know it backward and forward

The state laws on gifted education requirements in a school leader's state reveal the options for changes in a school. As repeatedly expressed, follow the law. Opportunities to serve students have a foundation set up by national, state and local law. A savvy school leader knows the law and relevant statutes and keeps them close in their "important documents" file. The next chapters outline other important documents to keep close.

Refer to these laws and statutes as school initiatives are developed for serving all students. Supervisors may not know the law or statutes. The school leader's power is in the use of their informed knowledge. Use the statutes as a starting point in building successful innovative programs.

Gifted program definitions and funding vary by state. The list below details how the state laws are applied to gifted education. A school leader needs to research their state's specific statutes to fully understand the foundations prior to implementing student-centered school initiatives. Only four states in the United States are fully funded. Yet, the onus of serving gifted students remains in the hands of the school district and the school leaders.

United States Gifted Education Laws by State: Retrieved Spring of 2020[18]

Mandated Gifted Programs	
Fully funded	FL, GA, IA, OK
Partially Funded	AL, AR, CO, HI, ID, IN, KS, KY, LA, ME, MI, MS, NE, NV, NM, NC, OH, SC, TN, TX, VA, WA, WV, WI
No Funding	AK, AZ, DE, IL, MD, MT, NJ, OR, PA, RI
Gifted Programs Not Mandated	
Partially Funded	CA, MO, ND, UT, WY
No Funding	CT, DC, MA, MN, NH, NY, SD, VT

(Davidson Institute)

Reading Discussion Questions:

1. Review the "Historical Legislative Events in Gifted Education" chart. Select one or more entries and explain how this legislation has had a direct impact on students identified as gifted in your school.
2. Discuss the gaps in these laws. Write a synopsis (or bullet points) of a legislative act which covers these gaps.
3. Determine the level of gifted program in your state. Research your state's Gifted Education laws on the state's Department of Education website. Copy and paste the definition of the program for future reference.

Closing

This section clarified the definition, needs, history and legislative support of the advanced learner. Ensuring equity in gifted education programs requires purposeful and informed efforts from school administrators. They have opportunities to capitalize on their understanding of the gifted student as they set the stage for the successful implementation of gifted initiatives showcased in the next sections.

School leaders and student advocates are often asked about their education philosophy. Or they are asked why they selected education as a career. The answer undoubtedly includes a statement regarding their belief that all students can learn and deserve to learn at the top of their ability.

As the halls fill with children in schools around the nation, is this true for all schools and every child? School leaders and student advocates have the power to make this belief a reality for their children. Gifted students are in every classroom waiting for their advocates to take a stand and create a culture of advanced learning. The successes of individual students depend on the school leader's selection of their own leadership style.

Part Two

The Purposeful Role of a School Leader in Meeting the Needs of All Advanced Learners.

There comes a time when one must take a position
that is neither safe, popular, or political;
but because it is right.

Dr. Martin Luther King, Jr.
(1929 – 1968, scholar & minister, leader of the Civil Rights Movement.
Awarded the Nobel Peace Prize in 1964)

Introduction to Part Two

These chapters provide the school leader with a pathway to meeting the needs of the advanced learner through shifting how the school infrastructure operates. These steps are critical to ensuring the needs of our highest achieving students are embedded in all aspects of the school's operation. There are intricate details and examples included to encourage school leaders to change current practices. The *Reading Discussion Activities* are directed toward future and current school leaders and their staff.

The *scenarios* are written from real-life experiences. How many times have we stated: "You can't make this stuff up!" The school leader will recognize these teachers, counselors, students, parents and school leaders. They are in every school, having the same thoughts about their experiences. The leader is responsible for their support. This is a big job. Know there is a village of peers who are available to assist in meeting their needs.

Parents of high achievers may find these processes interesting and utilize this information to advice or otherwise encourage administrators to make gifted student-centered decisions. However, the chapters in *Part Two* are getting into the "weeds" of school operations and may not be relevant to a parent's interests.

Parents of gifted children may be more comfortable skipping to *Part Three.* This last part is written for you through the experiences of school leaders. Explore these *Part Three* chapters at your leisure and know it is possible for all school leaders to actively and purposely serve our high level learners within a diverse school structure.

Chapter 4
The Ultimate Nurturing Academic Environment for the Advanced Learner

The infrastructure of a school has an impact on the gifted student's capacity to learn at their highest potential. This foundation includes how the master schedule is built, hiring practices, parental engagement and school counselor choices. These factors are purposefully addressed in this chapter to ensure student access to advanced support. This is not a matter of budget. It is a matter of the school leader's pragmatic organization and problem-solving priorities for these exceptional students.

If this is so simple, why is there an issue with gifted students receiving adequate resources and services? The focus of schools does not reside on the advanced learner. Our nation's educators are keenly aware of federal accountability. This drives a school leader's time, resources and constant focus. As a result, pressure on school leaders trickles down to their students. Scrutiny starts with kindergartners as they move to first grade and follows them to their senior year when they take high-stakes tests to graduate.

Each level of educator is judged by the reading and math learning gains of their lowest learning quartile. Because, first and foremost, it is the school's responsibility to graduate all students. These federal and state expectations encourage the school leader to focus on students under the federal microscope. This student data publicly reflects on the school leader's ability to lead a school.

Gifted students are likely to graduate on time. They silently exist off the radar of even the most celebrated school leaders. It *is* possible to fulfill the leader's promise to provide resources to all levels of learners. With purposeful actions, the school leader moves the needs of the gifted student onto their list of priorities while fulfilling their ultimate responsibility to graduate all students.

By just shifting a few resources...

This section will review how scarce resources are utilized to encourage all students to learn at the top of their academic ability. A school leader must shift their mindset to place students at every learning level in their focus. The first step is to recognize their current belief system regarding the gifted student.

Is it the most common belief that the students are self-sufficient? Academic performance conference requests made by parents or teachers are uncommon. Discipline-related phone calls are even more rare. Gifted students of all ages have the ability to disappear from authoritative figures to avoid unwanted attention. Once a leader acknowledges the low priority and little energy spent on serving the high achieving student, the process of building an infrastructure that includes serving all levels of learners can begin.

The learning gains of each student is the responsibility of the school leader. All children deserve to learn something new each school day. A student identified as gifted, as with all students, will experience school years that wax and wane with their own motivations and educational environment. However, the classroom environment, method of instruction and frequent review of student data can have a profound effect on increasing their ability to adapt and ultimately increase learning gains.

Observe the demographics of the students identified as gifted. Do they follow the overall demographics of the school's student population? If not, there is work to be completed.

Advanced learners are found in all tiers culturally, linguistically, economically and diversity. Students with disabilities are considered twice exceptional when identified as gifted. Building a diverse gifted population takes purposeful actions from the school leader.

The gifted mind experiences unique social and emotional needs. An alert school administrator or teacher will notice a change in their students' behavior and seek to find a solution which improves their social and academic experience. Veteran teachers of gifted students have a plethora of examples of their unique needs. Teaching students to adjust, cope and thrive requires attention, training and a willingness to adapt educational situations to the learner's needs.

Students need Champions in School Leadership

As a champion for the gifted, the school leader will encounter barriers to their gifted initiatives raised by entities inside and outside the school. The successful pursuit of excellence comes from a politically savvy problem-solver combined with a confident and driven leader. Remember the principles of the *leader versus manager* or *task versus visionary*. Listen politely to the naysayers as the school is built for all learners. Prepare to defend the resource shift by simply stating that the school has initiatives in place to successfully serve all students on the learning spectrum.

There is power in knowledge. Knowledge of the local, state and federal laws is imperative for a successful shift in school resources. Additionally, knowing the school district or the opinion of a supervisor on gifted education is important. Resources follow these opinions. This will not impact the change; it will only reveal the source of a potential barrier. The laws affect the allocation of funds which vary by state. *(Review the previous chapters for details on state and federal laws.)*

The information in Part Two provides the school leader and their team with tools to shift the school's infrastructure toward the successful inclusion of the advanced learner. The power of a leader is discovered as they meet the needs of all learners through pragmatic, cost-effective actions. Each chapter provides specific action items as well as rationale for the item's importance. The result is a detailed breakdown of how and why to make student-centered shifts within a school.

1. **The Master Schedule**

   The simple, yet strategically complex, organization of the course schedule drives how and where students learn. The decisive alignment of the courses with the student's needs provides an increase in choices and learning opportunities. The master schedule chapters provide an exploration of advanced options, minority student dynamics, the impact of electives, gifted programming models, the significance of a purposeful and organized registration process, and the many facets of scheduling staff.

2. **Hiring and Repurposing Staff**
   Human capacity on most campuses is built by the school leader as the ultimate hiring authority. Hiring, repurposing and terminating personnel directly impacts student learning. Practices are explored which will shift the school staff toward a gifted mindset through practical hiring practices, interview protocol and questions, teacher interventions and incentives. Various flexible strategies are provided in the training of all staff in educating gifted children. The federal Title II funds are frequently used for this purpose.
3. **Parent Advocates**
   Soldiers fighting for improved education are on the outside of schools and take the form of parents. They are a resource for the confident school leader. Parents have the ability to orchestrate change for all children as they seek to successfully navigate the school system for their own child. A toolbox of ideas is explored regarding how parents of gifted children and their school leaders can work together to build inclusive opportunities.
4. **School Counselor**
   On most school campuses, the gatekeepers at a school reside in the office of the counselor. These child advocates have control of assigned teachers and class schedules. Their time is their greatest and most limited resource. The non-negotiables for school counselors are revealed through defining their power to change the life of the gifted student.
5. **Defining a Gifted Student-Centered Education Environment**
   The decision to "not make a decision" to shift the focus to serving all students is making a decision to hinder the students

identified as gifted. A look at a school with only the required federal gifted programs reveals a stark reality of education negligence. This lens focuses on how the avoidance of small, simple shifts negatively impacts all children.

Champions of students are leading schools by tirelessly seeking information on meeting the needs of all levels of learners. Students who are high achieving have unique needs in both academics and social-emotional support. As stated, one of the nation's most valuable intellectual natural resources are these intelligently superior children. Foster their growth and watch them soar into highly productive adults.

The tools in the next chapters in Part Two provide school leaders with information and incentives on how to open the toolbox of gifted student supports. Now is the time to get to work on building a comprehensive educational environment. With the following chapters in hand, a school administration has a clear pathway to shift their leadership decisions to become actively involved in creating an inclusive school culture.

Reading Discussion Activities

1. Explain how your school's master schedule supports the inclusion of advanced learners.
2. Describe how school staff are hired and trained in meeting the needs of the high-level learners in your school.
3. Write three or more questions you have on how to better serve the gifted and talented student in your school.

Chapter 5

The School Leader's Obligation in Creating the Master Schedule

The architect of the master schedule has the ultimate power over school staff and student learning.

This statement is controversial to some school leaders. They are in disbelief that they need to take their time to build a schedule when a good assistant, counselor or a secretary has confidently completed this task in the past. If their reaction is *"I don't need to actually build it because I tell them what to put in the schedule and they do it."* Does the leader know the ramifications of their requests?

There is a void of information that can only be gleaned through the actual building process. A coach can tell a competitive runner if they want to win, they need to just run faster. To the runner, there is so much more involved mentally, physically and emotionally in preparation to win a race. The school leader has to experience every facet of building a schedule to understand its power in leading a school.

Another school administrator claims: *"We are using the same schedule we have used for years. If it's not broken, don't fix it."* This leader is claiming the children have not changed over the years. Each school year brings a new state course catalogue, changes in school district policies, teacher changes, and of course, a change in student interests. If the same schedule is used year after year, it is built for adults, not students.

Start the process with an organized purpose

The physical activity of building a school's master schedule reveals the hidden bones of a school. Look at this building process as an annual school data study. Build a spreadsheet.

Include this data on separate sheets or tabs of a school's master spreadsheet:

Student Individual Requirements (grade level, exceptionalities, elective requests, etc.)	Teachers & Certifications	Facilities (including physical classroom requirements)	Class & Time Schedule

Now, overlay each of these sheets. This is the most efficient master schedule. Note, that subjective reasoning is not considered in this model. There is no indication of a teacher's request for a specific classroom or grade level. These subjective requests are important. However, they are only considered after the most efficient student-based schedule is produced based on the data. This crucial document model is based on a "students first" mindset. The student requirements are in permanent ink, a locked spreadsheet, or another method of visualizing the importance of the student.

Knowing the student effects the master schedule

The creator of the master schedule who prioritizes the needs of the students cannot cut and paste it from a previous school year. Consider the current student population in American schools from kindergarten to 12th grade. Their academic environment has changed dramatically during their education on this 13-year spectrum. Their interests, academic sources, exceptionalities, and even their vernacular changes with each school year.

An efficient and effective master schedule reflects the uniqueness of each school year by meeting the needs of the *current* students. Additionally, in certain areas in the country, schools can have between one and six thousand students. It is the responsibility of the school leader to have an active role in positively impacting the school infrastructure through building the master schedule, hiring student-centered staff, supporting parents, and leading school counselors while considering the many facets of the gifted learner.

Below are the essentials elements to consider when building a master schedule:

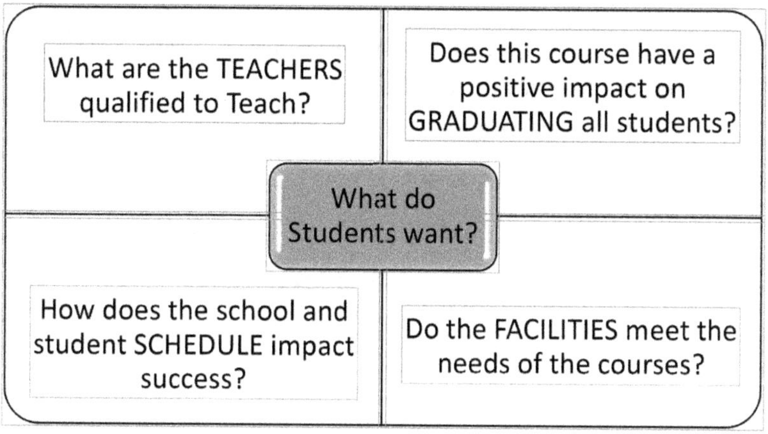

Within these critical elements are specific considerations to maintain a student-centered mindset. Each element includes an explanation and examples showcasing their relevance in the enhancement of education opportunities for the advanced learner. This information is valuable to the school leader who will bravely lay out the "bones," or data, of their school and personally build the master schedule.

Reading Discussion Activities

1. Explain in specific steps the school's master schedule building procedure. Include staff names and timelines.
2. Explain in specific steps the school's registration procedure. Include staff names and timelines.
3. Describe the specific strengths a school leader needs to plan and build a master schedule. The school leader needs knowledge of…a passion for…a resilience in…

Chapter 6
Never Underestimate the Power of Student Registration

Student course registration is the foundation of a student-centered master schedule. The registration of students for the upcoming school year provides the first data needed to build the schedule. A student's grade level and their specific needs are attached to their identity. For example, a second grader identified as gifted, who is twice exceptional with an immobility, will be scheduled into an appropriate classroom with easy access to a ramp or elevator. Or the middle schooler who is identified as gifted and has an Individual Education Plan (IEP), which includes a requirement for small group learning, is placed in a classroom which meets this exceptionality. A high school student identified as gifted may have an English language accommodation and require a schedule with a cohort of similar students with fluency support requirements.

"Give me six hours to chop down a tree and I will spend the first four sharpening the axe."
—Abraham Lincoln

Taking time to prepare a registration sheet will glean the data needed to build a student-centered master schedule. These critical pre-registration steps are covered in detail within the following sections. Preparing for student registration that meets all levels of learners is comparable to Abraham Lincoln sharpening his ax.

The registration procedures for Elementary Grades

The elementary student identified as gifted may be two or three grade levels ahead of their age-appropriate class in a specific subject. It is common for a gifted student to have an acuity for at least one subject. The encouragement of continued acceleration within this subject is essential for the continued development of the child.

Students without such support eventually lose their acuity in their chosen subject. The Acceleration Institute at the Belin-Blank Center states that failing to accelerate has negative effects. Students remaining in under-challenging learning environments are less likely to fully develop their giftedness.[1]

The student learning above grade level experiences boredom and potential behavior problems if not challenged in their classroom. A solution is to schedule the student in an appropriate class which teaches their accelerated subject at the same time of day as an upper grade. For example, the gifted student's second-grade teacher instructs math daily from 9:00 a.m. to 9:50 a.m. The master schedule accommodates the gifted student's need for acceleration by scheduling the fourth-grade teacher's math block at the same time of day. The student travels to the accelerated classroom for math instruction. The student's math acceleration need is attached to their identity and "locked" together as a scheduling priority. Elementary services are often provided by a multi-grade pull-out enrichment period meeting two to three times a week. This practice serves as an addition to the "enrichment only" model.

***10th grader**: I hated registering for classes in middle school. It was pointless. There were not very many choices and they were the same every year. But at my high school, the registration sheet is cool and easy to use. I know what I have to take because all my required courses are already filled out for me. This is my registration sheet. It has my name on it. Check it out! I can see how picking this one class will impact next year. Also, I'm really good at science. I'm going to skip the next level and go to a senior level science class. It's all here on my sheet. Cool, huh?*

The registration procedures for Secondary Grades

The registration documents for both middle and high school students should be personalized. Even the largest middle and high schools have this ability through software programs. Each student receives a form with their name and student identification number at the top. Their registration document reflects their specific requirements for graduation, accommodations, recommendations for advanced courses, required remediation courses, the next class in their elective sequence, etc. This personalization relieves stress for the student and their parent by providing a clear and informed choice of their course options. Without personalization, a parent may feel they need to fight for their student's accelerated option, elective or additional course selection.

The middle school registration procedures

The middle school student who accelerates in math can experience the same scheduling solution. For example, a sixth grader entering a new middle school identified as gifted and needing acceleration in math can be placed into a seventh or eighth grade class to continue their trajectory of advancement. This type of acceleration may leave the student with few math options as they enter their last year of middle school. An articulation agreement with the local high school or online courses taken independently are considerations. These acceleration options outside of a regular school schedule are provided in the acceleration section below.

The middle school registration document should include grade level core classes as well as a plethora of electives. Depending on the school, the core classes are mathematics, science, language arts, and social science. Many middle years programs require physical education, reading, technology or other courses at specific grade levels.

This age of student is springing out into the secondary environment wanting to learn beyond what was provided by the narrow elementary academic curriculum. The personalized registration document includes recommendations for advanced core subjects, required courses by grade level, and the courses which meet their exceptionality requirements.

High school registration procedures

The registration of high school students provides a vast amount of options. It is easiest for counselors or registrars to place enrolled students into their predetermined grade level core classes and provide them with a limited choice of grade specific electives. This is not building a master schedule by prioritizing students.

Scheduling high school students with advanced needs is as simple as meeting their academic requirements through non-grade-level placement. Place the student into the course that meets their academic abilities. Yes, the grades will be mixed, and their sequence of courses will be compromised.

This unique learner will thrive when properly scheduled. These advanced learners will either be challenged or "go along to get along" for the grade. The school leader needs to know the difference through observation of the advanced learners and their individual data.

A differentiated classroom can meet the needs of gifted learners. However, teachers need training in how to take the material to a deeper level of complexity while encouraging advanced skills. There are multiple studies which support the successes of both homogeneous and heterogeneous groupings of high achievers. It comes down to teacher training. A great teacher with the knowledge of how to stretch a child's learning process while also serving those who are competent in the less challenging curriculum, brings learning to all levels.

Accelerated course options are identified as Honors, Advanced Placement, college courses, and other institutional options such as International Baccalaureate or Cambridge. An explanation of these options is outlined in the acceleration section.

Actively explore the power of listing electives on a registration sheet

The registration of students into electives carries the weight of both interest and emotional dynamics. The administrator builds the master schedule by, first, filling the core content requirements for every enrolled student. The electives receive the remaining resources of teachers and class periods. *The importance of elective offerings is not to be underestimated by the school leader.*

For elementary schools, the number of teachers per grade level is determined by the number of students enrolled by grade level. Elementary schedules have fewer elective choices for students within the school day. The students are generally required to take the "special" with their class to allow their core teacher a planning period. Electives usually include a variation of music, physical education, art and technology. When organizing "specials" in the master schedule, take into consideration that the high achieving student may be learning subjects in a higher grade-level classroom which has their "special" scheduled at a different time from their peer grade level.

For secondary schools, the available electives are frequently based on staff availability and qualifications. The core courses and graduation requirements take precedent over electives. For example, a secondary English teacher may also teach the school yearbook classes. If the student population for the school year grows or needs a specific certification, the teacher may lose one of the yearbook classes. The core has priority because it is a graduation requirement. Furthermore, the availability of a course in a high school can have a direct impact on graduation requirements. A wise school leader will allow their school counselors to review these elements of the master schedule.

Secondary electives should be based on student interest. The registration sheet will include courses which have yet to have an assigned teacher. For example, place computer science on the elective sheet to determine student interest. If more than a class size of students selects this option, find a teacher. If an elective course has a history of only a few interested students, cancel the course. Teachers of electives have the responsibility of selling their course to the students.[2]

The nuances of electives for gifted students

Elective course selection for the advanced learner takes place with great purpose and thought. They are attracted to academic, non-academic, college level and career pathway options. Gifted students have both academic and social scheduling needs.

Social concerns reside with mixing grade levels, the assignment to specific teachers, clustered with like-students, and being separated from troublesome students based on past experiences. Each scheduling decision is taken with the student's perspective as a priority. A detailed description of the advanced student's needs and thought processes are provided in the elective selection section.

The American school system is set up by scheduling kindergarten through twelfth grade students based on their age, not their ability. A few tweaks in the master schedule opens up the possibilities of students taking classes with their intellectual peers. Student registration based on the priority of student needs and wants will start the master schedule with a solid academic foundation on which to add qualified staff, facility requirements and constraints of the school day.

Influencing course selection opens doors for students

A savvy school leader influences course election prior to registration. The elements below are pivotal considerations when selecting courses and programs for students of all learning levels. This is where the rubber meets the road for serving students first. Each element directly affects a child's experience in a school.

An informed school leader will seek to make a positive impact on students with each step of this process. The documents, used mainly in middle and high school, may appear as a small part of the master schedule building process. But they are sources of information that, if used properly, increase student engagement for all levels of learners. Place the responsibility of creating these documents in the hands of the staff member who understands their power. Monitor and change any element which is not adding to a student-first, positive school culture.

A hands-on administrator may receive pushback from the previous creator of the master schedule. They know the builder holds a high level of importance to the school operations. These leadership shifts take thought, planning, energy, resiliency and even tenacity.

Most students have a renewed expectation of a positive registration experience each school year. By placing the selection process into the hands of the student, they have ownership of their school experiences. Creating an atmosphere of celebration during the registration process jump starts the future school year. The leader starts the preparation calendar with a positive culture.

Research teacher credentials prior to registration: determine impact on student needs

The spreadsheet reflecting the enrolled student's *needs* for the new school year is in place. Each student has a list of their required courses, exceptionality accommodations, potential elective preferences, etc. Now is the time to determine what staff is needed to fulfill these requirements.

The *teacher spreadsheet* or a preferred hardcopy document will include the following three items. This is a purposely short list. Building a student-centered master schedule requires that the teachers fit the needs and desires of the students.

	Certification, Credentials & Endorsements to teach or support	**Desired Assignment includ-ing Grade Level, Subject & Planning**	**Special Notes**
Teacher name			
Teacher name			
Teacher name			

Be aware that if the teacher has been in place longer than the school leader has worked at the school, there may be an assumption that the teacher is only qualified for the grade level or course they currently teach. By researching the credentials of every staff member through the recording entity (state department of education or other governing authority) the credential is revealed and recorded. For example, the elementary music teacher may have credentials in music, reading, a gifted endorsement and specific grade levels. This knowledge provides the administrator with more options to schedule students.

Secondary teacher credentials are commonly earned in a subject area. The astute teacher will gain multiple subject qualifications to enhance their employability. Consequently, the school leader has the ability to place the qualified teacher into a variety of courses. A caveat is the policy of the school, district or union may limit a teacher's assigned subjects.

An efficient master schedule will layer the qualified teacher's responsibilities. For example, an eighth-grade teacher who is certified in both social science and gifted education may be assigned to teach an all-gifted American History class. The schedule and content requirements for gifted accommodations or support are met through their core subject material.

> ***Secondary Teacher**: I have taught 10th grade World History for 6 years. I am so burned out. Each year they automatically put me in this course even after new social science teachers are hired. I guess they just assume this is my course. It was not until my principal noticed I have credentials to teach gifted students and I was offered a different course. I'm excited about the change. I know it will be a challenge to start from scratch. But I am ready.*

Distinguish between the staff with or without a gifted mindset

A school leader is wise to scan their teaching staff and determine who may have the affective strengths to teach gifted students. Teachers with a heart for the gifted student may only need encouragement to pursue and complete a gifted teaching credential. Depending on the district or state policies, this teacher may teach gifted children while earning their credential.

Experienced teachers of students identified as gifted claim their assignment is not as easy as it seems. Teaching the "smart kids" includes challenges not felt by other teachers. Gifted students may have a deep knowledge of certain subjects, require behavior interventions to excel and learn quickly how to excite a teacher. Effective teachers learn to remain confident when they are not the expert in the classroom.

On the other end of the spectrum is the ineffective teacher assigned to gifted students. This generally occurs when the teacher has held this class for multiple school years or has "earned" the right to teach the "smart kids" because of their veteran teacher status. It is the assumption of the teacher and the school that this is their historical assignment. A legacy assignment, per se. The spreadsheet with teacher names, credentials, desired course and grade level will reflect the teachers with gifted credentials. By selecting a qualified new gifted teacher from the current staff, the administrator is making a decision to serve students over adults.

Facility considerations impact the master schedule prior to student registration

An administrator starts with a map of the school which includes the classrooms, subject-specific classrooms, exceptionality classrooms, and even bathrooms and closets. Reflect on the previous school years. Were the placements of the grade levels and course subjects student centered? It is obvious that a science and math classroom have different physical requirements from a physical education, music or vocational classroom. Outside of these facility requirements, the administrator has options in the placement of the students into their core and elective classes.

The school leader will review the facilities and determine the purposeful location of classrooms. Classes in elementary school are generally clustered by grade level. This is efficient for both the student and the teachers. The kindergarteners should not cross paths with the big fifth graders. There are few choices outside moving entire grade levels. Note, the gifted student who must travel to an upper grade level class will cross into the territory of older students. This student can be supported with encouragement and monitoring.

Middle schools are also commonly organized by grade level. The core subjects are taught in adjacent classrooms by grade level. Sixth graders mix with each other and the eighth or ninth graders enjoy their elevated status in separate hallways.

The high school leader has an opportunity to impact the school culture by altering the master schedule by clustering subjects. Serve students first in the school by regarding their interests when scheduling classes. The clustering of students by their chosen elective is one example of serving the student's academic and social needs in high school. This method groups students by their interests, not their grade level.

Specialty courses demand special classrooms.

Many high schools have learning pathways. Business, technology, agricultural science, medical, culinary, construction, early college and music are examples of common high school elective pathways. The students take a sequence of courses in their chosen pathway starting in the ninth or tenth grade.

A student-centered master schedule will place all grades of students taking a common pathway in one area of the campus. For example, students who share the business pathway will take their core classes in the same area. This scheduling method provides an extraordinary opportunity for high achieving students. The advanced student learning above grade level will thrive with their multi-grade peers in both elective and core classes. Conversely, students who need remediation will also be placed with their pathway peers.

Adapting leadership decisions in the assignment of classrooms to serve students first is an important step in the master schedule building process. Keep in mind that the gifted student learns at a higher level when working with groups of both differentiated and wholly gifted students.[3] What does this classroom look like? Traditional classrooms place students into neat rows facing forward to accommodate the need to monitor behavior and see lectures given at the front of the classroom. Even computer screens are often positioned to face the teacher to help monitor behavior.

A classroom designed to meet the needs of students will have grouped tables or desks. This arrangement induces conversation, collaboration and cooperation. Understand that this is known as a noisy design.

If used as a gifted pullout or exclusively gifted classroom with project-based-learning, locate the classroom away from noise sensitive classes. It will be noisy. Teacher training is essential regarding methods for teaching in the student-centered classroom with clustered desks.

Recognize how a gifted student selects their electives during registration

Information is added to the secondary school registration sheets regarding prerequisites, required special permissions, and caveats indicating there is a possibility that the courses may not be offered. Instruct students to select ten electives identified with a number prioritizing their interests. Course descriptions are located on the school website along with other valuable selection criteria relevant to specific courses and the selection process.

An advanced learner looks at a registration sheet with a discerning eye. Behind the course title are multiple important variables which will appeal or repel the gifted student:

Positives	**Negatives**
The teacher	The teacher
Fair grading practices	Difficult to earn an "A"
Homework is limited & relevant	Homework is busywork
Challenging problem-solving	No rigor, class is too easy
Works in groups during class	Poor classroom management
Content is appealing to interests	Irrelevant content to interests
More advanced learners in class	No peers are in the class

Most of these positive and negative attributes are learned through peer conversations and may vary in truthfulness. Regardless of credibility, the advanced student shops for the best opportunity by carefully considering all variables. Many of these conversations will take place on social media and at the Registration Fair. An example of a *Registration Fair Set Up and Agenda* is provided as *Appendix A.* Note this is an agenda for a school wide high school Registration

Fair and is not specific to Gifted Education. This example provides a template for a school leader to design and implement a fair which ensures Gifted Education is included.

Develop a Data Rich Registration Sheet after Gathering Student and Teacher Data

In the previous section, we revealed how important the student registration process is in building a master schedule. Let's take a deeper dive into this powerful document. What it looks like, how it is organized and what courses are pivotal to building each year's schedule of classes. This document has the potential to be a student's pathway to success. A well-thought-out registration document will provide the school leader with the data needed to make decisions on how to meet the needs of the students. It will reveal their interests. A leader should take their opinions into account when scheduling classes.

Make the registration sheet look cool.

It is a unique color with the school logo at the top. These registration sheets are commonly used in middle and high school. Elementary registration is centered on grade level courses. Of course, the gifted student receives consideration for placement into upper grade-level opportunities within the school. There are non-negotiable, or required, core classes printed on the personalized registration sheet. Little student time and energy is spent on these courses.

The advanced student's active selection of courses involves several variables. First, every student wants to take classes with their friends. They communicate and work toward building a homogeneous schedule. The administrator can use this knowledge to increase enrollment in pathways or specific electives.

Adding electives such as poetry, world languages and multiple types of applied technology to the registration sheet prior to finding a teacher will provide the administrator with data on student interest. If a teacher is not found after aggressive searching, these subjects can be made into afterschool clubs. This is a win-win for the students. The gifted student who does not have room in their schedule for robotics, will actively participate in an after-school club with like-minded students.

An example of a freshman core course registration sheet for an advanced learner is included as *Appendix B.1.* This student is in a four-year International Baccalaureate school. The junior and senior years are known as the International Baccalaureate Diploma Program. An additional example of the back of a sophomore elective registration sheet is included as *Appendix B.2.* The freshman and sophomore years are a preparation for these rigorous courses. This example is a template and may be adapted to any level of learner with diverse coursework.

The course progressions are clearly listed on the registration sheet. By including these course sequences, the student has knowledge of courses that are available in their future. Additionally, an advanced student may petition to take a more rigorous course outside of their past course sequences. The sequence of core courses is obvious: English 1, English 2, English 3, English 4. However, elective courses do not always have an obvious sequence: Computer Science Principles, Computer Operating System Security, Cyber Security 1, Cyber Security II. By listing the courses, the advanced student can explore advanced options.

Personalized registration sheets for each student

The personalized elementary registration sheet is adapted by grade level. Starting with kindergarten, parents appreciate the list of subjects covered in their young scholar's school day. Kindergarteners receive a one-page sheet with each core and elective, or "special", listed along with calendars or other important communication.

The first through third graders receive a personalized registration sheet which includes all three grades. Fourth and fifth graders receive their own personalized registration sheet with the two grades. The additional grades provide information on the progression of the core and elective classes. Parents will communicate their preferences and questions to school leaders by using the sequence or availability of electives outside the grade level. The qualified gifted student and their parent have a more informed picture of what is available outside of their grade level. This may be a novel concept for staff and parents at the elementary level.

The personalized middle school registration sheet includes the core and elective courses for the three grade levels (or 4 grade levels if applicable). The bright-eyed sixth graders will enjoy looking at the courses for all three grades. Their selection of electives is more informed with knowledge of the course progression. The seventh and eighth graders will identify their interests by providing their administrator with their elective selections. Remember, list electives which may not have an assigned teacher or classroom. This is an interest survey to use to build a positive school culture and a master schedule that is based on the student interests and not built for adult convenience.

The personalized high school registration sheet is a multiple page packet of information. Again, all grade levels are present. The core course progressions on the students' personalized registrations sheets are highlighted by their grade level.

The secondary school leader has several choices of how to organize the elective options. If the high school is organized into pathways, it is important to cluster the elective courses by pathway. For example: Medical, Technology, Business, Agriscience, etc. If there are no programs of study, the electives are organized by subject. For example: world languages, physical education, technology, etc. There are elective courses available in the core subjects of science, language arts, social sciences and mathematics. Every elective course is listed in additional to courses which are a survey of the student interest.

A Comprehensive Registration Process Will Positively Impact Course Selection

Virtual school registration sheets are a great place to start. Publish each registration sheet on the school website with detailed course descriptions. Links to videotaped teacher explanations will give students a peek at the teacher's personality. Completing the entire registration process virtually is possible, but not advisable. Look at students as clients. They want to be sold the courses by their engaging and informative teachers.

A Registration Fair brings separate grade levels together to explore the available electives. Middle and high school students enjoy visiting each elective booth to learn about the course expectations. Questions are answered by the teacher with current or former students. The booth's ancillary items showcase the class with tangible products and multimedia. The student leaves the Registration Fair with a better understanding of what is expected in the class. School counselors and administrators are available to answer questions and give permissions to accelerate into a course outside a student's grade level.

The student submits their final registration sheet online. The data is gathered and segregated into course requests. The school leader receives a spreadsheet of student interests and starts working on meeting their expectations by hiring or repurposing teachers, changing classrooms to meet facility requirements, and starting clubs for non-viable courses.

Reading Discussion Activities

1. Describe a perfect registration sheet from the child's perspective. Sketch it out with descriptions of what is important for the student. Place numbers by priority of the most important parts of the registration sheet to the student.
2. Write a timeline for your school's registration process. Include assigned tasks and deadlines.
3. Write an action plan for your school's Registration Fair. Select a date, a location, the format, a layout of the facilities, staff involved, assigned tasks for implementation, etc.

Chapter 7
A School Leader Knows the Answers:
Core & Elective Courses and All Things Master Schedule

The core courses in kindergarten through twelfth grade are determined by a state board of education. Their selection and sequencing are determined by educators with professional knowledge of the content and child development. National standards give states their box in which to reside while creating these state standards.

Each level of administrator should have a working knowledge of the state's unique graduation and grade promotion requirements. It is unfortunate that teachers frequently have a better understanding of their course descriptions, sequencing and standards than their administrators.

Here are some simple actions to keep the school leader in the loop of curriculum requirements.

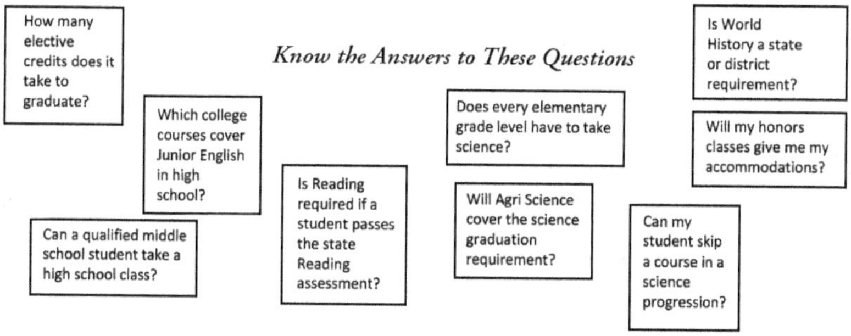

Keep important documents at hand. Saving the state and school district official academic curriculum policy documents for easy access is recommended. These documents are updated each school year and can be saved as printed hardcopies or saved as an icon on a computer desktop.

1. State adopted core and elective courses
2. State adopted career and technical education courses
3. State adopted requirements for remediation
4. Students with exceptionalities policy and procedures
5. School district's recommended course progression documents
6. School district's student progression plan
7. Teacher union contract
8. The school's curriculum guide with course descriptions and progressions
9. All testing dates and deadlines
10. Calendar expectations for school, district and state

These valuable documents will answer questions that will arise when building a master schedule. The reliance on the school counselor or assistant principal to know this information will take away the school leader's ability to build an effective student-centered master schedule. Remember, it is easier to follow the previous school year's protocol or delegate complicated tasks. "Easy" does not serve the current students. Creativity and problem-solving class schedules with current student data will boost school's culture and give the leader powerful information.

Elementary Core caveats for advanced learners

Elementary students follow a core curriculum based on their grade level, which is based on their age. Depending on the school, there are few opportunities to break out of this structure. "Staying on grade level" is a claim made by teachers and their supervisors. The students learning "below grade level" are provided intervention activities. Students learning "above grade level" are frequently given additional assignments.

The flexible elementary school leader has the opportunity to review the student data and place students accordingly. A student who is learning between one and three grades above their peers needs exposure to a rigorous curriculum outside of the age-based grade level.

A flexible and creative leader finds a schedule which aligns with the student's learning acuity. The student may travel to an upper grade level and fully participate in the lesson for their accelerated subject. The master schedule takes the needs of the student into account by placing the same core subjects at the same time, in each grade level. Another option is to schedule the student into an online class which meets the desired rigor. Supervision in a media center, office, etc. is arranged through the administrator.

Secondary Core caveats for advanced learners

The core curriculum in a middle or junior high is similar to the elementary courses based on grade level, which is based on age. Larger schools may have the capacity to split classes into learning levels. For instance, students scheduled into a sixth-grade math requirement may be separated based on their fifth-grade test scores or their identification as *gifted*. This practice provides a track for the regular student and a track for the advanced learner.

Accelerated practices in middle schools, regardless of size, have the potential of scheduling students based on their abilities. For instance, a subject-specific pre-test can be given to each grade level to measure academic knowledge. Considerations for course placement are determined by this subject-specific pre-test, previous teacher recommendation, previous test scores, and other available student achievement data. The students are clustered into classes which reflect their academic data, not their age.

The high achieving middle schooler may have taken the highest academic classes in the school prior to entering eighth grade. The school leader finds a solution for the student's next courses. By starting high school courses in middle school, the problem is solved. Accessibility to these courses is the next problem needing a solution.

There are several possibilities to consider. First, a high school credentialed middle school teacher providing the course through an independent study. Second, the student takes the course from an approved online source. Lastly, the student may travel to the high school to take the class. There are many high school courses that can be offered on middle school campuses. Nevertheless, this does not eliminate the possibility that high achieving students often successfully complete these courses prior to eighth grade.

The middle school years are some of the most difficult learning times in a child's life. The "Smart Kid" is no longer at the top of their class. Now, there are even smarter kids they have not met from other elementary schools. The middle school leader must create a successful academic experience in the first year. This is where students meet "their people."

Campus clubs should be diverse and include a safe place to blend with peer groups. Make it cool to be smart. Gifted middle school students may look and act quite different from other students. Thankfully, fellow gifted students accept them due to their respect for their gift of intellect. Actively protect these self-conscious students from peers, other parents and staff.

The high school core courses in a master schedule are complex and may seem overwhelming until the layers are peeled away. The primary responsibility of a high school is to graduate students. Knowledge of the state graduation requirements is like a football coach's knowledge of the playbook. The accessibility of core graduation requirements drives the leadership decisions.

All requirements are completed by the end of the student's four-year attendance of high school. These requirements are taken at any time during the student's tenure. If a student fulfills the basic requirements in 10th grade, then be ready with options for him to continue learning on or off campus.

11th Grade Gifted Student: *I received my senior registration sheet and noticed that I have taken every math course offered at my school and the local college. I love math and I am good at it. I asked my counselor what to do at the Registration*

Fair. We went to my principal and let her know I was out of math options. It took about 3 weeks, but she let me know she received permission from her boss and South University to take their dual enrollment. I am excited about taking an engineering-based math course at the university during my senior year.

The traditional high school scheduling model is similar to other grades. Students are placed in grades based on their age. With the offering of high school courses in middle schools becoming more common, these age-based practices are going the way of the buggy whip. Administrators are called to evaluate the needs of incoming high school students by what they need to graduate and not a canned schedule given to every entering freshman. This will throw off a school who uses a master schedule built many years prior to the current school year. An effective registration process gives school leaders the student data needed to build a high school master schedule with the correct core subjects.

Students identified as gifted prior to their high school years are not automatically successful in high school. Their success is dependent on their past learning experiences. A student who received high grades in every class without a challenging curriculum may experience a "set back" in high school. The advanced learner must learn how to study. Nurturing teachers will guide these bright students to this goal.

Furthermore, it is unrealistic to expect students with advanced learning abilities to perform at high levels if they have not been exposed to opportunities to learn at advanced levels. This exposure teaches the student "how to learn" new material. The school leader will discern and provide additional encouragement and support to advanced students who need help "learning how to learn".[1]

The Various Core Credit Options for Accelerating the Gifted Secondary Student

A gifted student wants to experience rigorous courses. Teachers want to teach interesting courses. This is a natural bridge if the administrator researches courses which articulate. This research is a valuable use of time in the preparation of listing courses on the registration sheet. A thorough evaluation of alternative core classes will include teacher credential and facility requirements.

Acceleration beyond a grade-level course

Students entering high school with high school credits in core courses are scheduled into the next grade level. For example, the eighth grader who completes freshman English will be accelerated into the sophomore English course their freshman year. Similar situations occur when gifted middle school students take algebra 1, geometry or algebra 2. Upper class mathematics are their high school options. The ages are mixed with students of the same academic level.

Alternative cores subjects: research course directories

A glance at the state adopted courses gives a plethora of options to the most common core requirements. For example, a graduation requirement is the completion of Earth Space Science. Research into the code directory reveals Agriscience 1 meets the Earth Space Science requirement. The high school has an Agriscience Pathway or Academy. With this knowledge, the school leader can place the incoming freshman, who selected this pathway on their registration sheet, into the Agriscience 1 course. This creates a co-hort of like-minded freshmen who meet their freshman science requirement for graduation. Furthermore, the advanced student who took Earth Space Science in middle school may opt to take this more relevant science course with this co-hort of learners. This is just one example. There are many core equivalents in the state course guide.

Testing Out: positives and negatives

Students are often given the option to "test out" of a core course in high school. The advanced student must consider some caveats prior to making this decision. First, never test out of a course which has an amazing teacher. These top teachers are rare and have gained their reputations by not only knowing their content, but by valuing their students. The gifted student will learn more than just the content from these top tier teachers.

Additionally, a high school transcript may reflect a course that was waived by passing a test. Universities are fickle about testing out of required courses. Ask the student or their parent to call the admissions office of their targeted university prior to testing out of a course. Furthermore, universities value a rigorous four-year high school schedule. A student who completes their core graduation requirements in eleventh grade or earlier is advised to take alternative core subjects for the remaining high school year(s). Alternatives are a science from a different pathway, a college literature class, an applied mathematics or social science course that will meet this criterion.

Advanced Placement or college courses?

Most states assign their high school courses a credit weight: Regular is 1.0, honors are 1.5, Advanced Placement and college-level courses are 2.0. These credits are added to create a grade point average reflecting the rigor of the courses. Competitive college bound students shop for courses with the highest credit weight.

The school leader meets their needs by making higher-weighted courses available. Students may skip a freshman or sophomore level course which is unweighted and start with a weighted upper level course. If teacher availability is an issue, an option is to remove core honors courses and replace them with an Advanced Placement equivalent, such as offering only Regular English and Advanced Placement Literature or Language. This practice may cause issues at the end of the school year when students may not be prepared to take the Advanced Placement exams.

College level core courses can be taken by advanced students in lieu of the regular course progression. The caveats to this practice are the student's final grade. It is now included in a part of their permanent college record. They must take these classes seriously. A non-high school class is not in the jurisdiction of the high school leader. The college oversees the grading, homework, content, teacher and other critical variables.

It is important to consult with the admissions at the targeted university before substituting a high school course with a core college course. For example, English 4 can be replaced with a semester of

College Freshman English. However, the universities may prefer an advanced student take a course with a normed test, such as Advanced Placement, Cambridge or International Baccalaureate. The results of the test will indicate the material learned. The course content of an early college course does not have a common normed assessment.

A plethora of acceleration options take place outside the walls of the school. Some of these options are paid for by parents. Most are known as highly credible throughout the advanced learner communities. Students of any age enjoy working on their assignments during the school day and after school. The Belin-Blank Center offers the Iowa Online Advanced Placement Academy (IOAPA). A sampling of online and distant learning options is below.[2]

- Hoagies' Gifted Education Page, High School Courses & Curriculum Materials: http://www.hoagiesgifted.org/online_hs.htm
- Hoagies' Gifted Education, Distance Learning: http://www.hoagiesgifted.org/distance_learning.htm
- Northwestern CTD, Online Programs: http://www.ctd.northwestern.edu/program_type/online-programs
- John Hopkins Center for Talented Youth, Online Programs: http://cty.jhu.edu/ctyonline/

Elective Choices Impact the Lives of the Gifted Student

Electives are required to graduate. Elementary, middle and high school students select electives for a variety of reasons. Their own interests may carry the same value as which friends will join them in the class. The choice of which electives to offer is dependent on the student interests.

Elective courses have an ability to change a child's future by exposing them to a thorough understanding of a subject. Robotics courses can produce engineers. Medical courses can produce doctors. Business courses can produce entrepreneurs. World language courses produce international ambassadors. School leaders should encourage all students to take electives relevant to their interests.

> ***10th Grade Gifted Student:*** *I picked an elective I was interested in when I entered high school as a freshman. The first class was mixed with upper classmen. I was a little intimidated by the seniors. It was awesome when we started doing projects. We do everything in groups. Juan doesn't speak much English, but, man, can he write code. These are my friends. We all think the same. My principal said I have found "my people." She is right. All of us are different. But we speak the same language: Robotics!*

The gifted student thrives in electives. If scheduled with their interests as a priority, they will be with "their people" as the scenario suggests. These shared interests provide a safe place to show their intellect and take academic risks. An effective registration sheet delivers data to the master schedule builder on which electives to offer. Electives that receive insufficient student selections are considered for cancelation.

With an understanding of the courses approved by the state and district, a school leader will skillfully fill the canceled elective spots with popular courses. These replacement courses may need a small innovative adjustment. For example, students may not register for Computer Repair, yet they will crowd into Robotics. The content and teacher certification are similar. The course name is simply more attractive to the student.

Most high-level learners are grade motivated. By purposefully scheduling electives which cater to their interests, their grade point averages will soar. Additionally, if a student has a lesser ability in a required core course, the elective letter grades will offset the lower core grade on their grade point average.

Students identify with their elective choices

There are the Band Kids, the Business Kids, the Agriscience Kids, etc. These are small learning communities which add to the feeling of belonging in a school community. They "complete" each other. These are "their people." This collaborative family atmosphere leads to a has a higher achievement, a fulfilled social life, and ultimately, an increase in parent involvement.

The administrator should obtain thorough knowledge about the interests and needs of their underserved student populations. These are underrepresented students and students living in poverty. Purposefully selected electives can have a powerful impact on improving attendance. Consider the time of day the electives are offered. Many underserved children use the school or city bus for transportation and cannot stay after school for clubs or other school events. Protect the needs of these students by monitoring the elective teacher's requirements for after school or weekend activities.

Staff these electives with flexible, yet rigorous teachers. Make it a policy to not require students to pay fees for any course. Find the funds to support these classes through fundraisers, internal budgets or other means.

The administrator who knows the power of elective choices on a student's learning will place the students' needs over the adults' needs in a school. It is a problem if a popular elective is scheduled at the same time as a singleton (only offered one time in a school day or week). This is another reason the school leader must make difficult decisions to serve their most popular electives and their teachers. For example, if Band is a highly prized subject for students, ensure the Band class period is scheduled where and when the band teacher requests it and not at the same time as a required core course.

Mixing students of all learning and grade levels in Electives

Should different levels of learners be clustered together in electives? Absolutely! The student data which identifies a student's learning level in reading or math does not consider how a student may respond in a desired elective. Interest stimulates learning. Age is irrelevant as students with common interests thrive together in creating solutions to common problems in their shared specialty's. Provide a low-level reader interested in auto mechanics with a schematic on how to fix a car and watch them soar. Additionally, mixed grade levels in electives will foster a mentor/mentee community of learners.

Mixing ability levels in electives is supported by the relevant and little-discussed *Frog Pond Theory* which relates to ability grouping for adults as well as children. This effect occurs because students focus on their relative performance standing within their group rather than on their group's overall performance level..[3] Frog Pond Theory is used with both homogeneous and heterogeneous groupings of students to stretch grade-motivated competitive students to the top of their abilities.[4]

The frog pond is a small learning community. Each member within the community participates and thrives at their desired level. Their motivation to earn recognition through grades or other measurements is based on the other members in the "frog pond." A competitive student will meet the criteria to be the top scholar in the "pond" or class. If the pond is filled with low to average learners, the competitive student will only be motivated to be at the top of the "average" spectrum. There is no motivation to enter the "above average" range if they can be at the top of the class on the "average" spectrum. Place the competitive student into a class of low, average and high-level learners and they will be motivated to climb to the top of the high-level spectrum.

Age-based scheduling in electives is to be avoided for the benefit of all levels of learners. Mixed ability levels within electives foster communities of collaboration among peers with like interests. Watch as some of the younger students, not identified as advanced learners, thrive in classes with gifted students. Their acuity for the elective may rival their older gifted peers in a high level of understanding in history, technology, psychology, science, math, etc. By placing this student with the gifted students, the Frog Pond is alive with new competition.

The school leader who places students first when building a master schedule will take time each school year to study the vast elective course offerings approved by the state. Research other schools in the district, state and even the nation to learn what is popular. Review the possibility of creating pathways or programs of study. Look at the scholarship and award results of good competitive electives and how this positively impacts a school culture.

Think "outside the box" of previously offered electives. Ask teachers and other staff to brainstorm ideas on elective offerings. Know they have already discussed these possibilities. Research the school communities and listen to the ideas of your staff. Then, place these new electives on the registration sheet and wait for the student-interest data to indicate which to offer.

Considering Acceleration options while building a gifted student-centered master schedule

School leaders determine how to raise student achievement through the implementation of accelerated options in a school. Programming options vary by school for gifted and talented students. Research demonstrates the most effective options are pullout programs, specialized classes and cluster-grouped classes and regular classrooms.[5] These various options are considered while building a master schedule.

Elementary students identified as gifted need challenging academic environments to continue to excel through future school years. Federal and state statutes are often met through pullout specials and self-contained gifted classrooms. Teachers may differentiate classrooms with clustered groupings, tiered assignments and extension menus. Extended learning opportunities naturally occur outside the classroom when leaders and teachers initiate clubs built on student interests. It is in elementary school when most discussions occur for skipping grade levels.[6] These decisions come with the obvious social impacts and should be carefully considered. The IOWA Acceleration Scales serves as a guide for parents and educators to make decisions on grade acceleration.[7]

Secondary students identified as gifted thrive in a common environment. As referenced by the Frog Pond Theory, gifted students need to be challenged to push their academic limits. This acceleration process can be accomplished through allowing students into ability-based courses not age-based courses. Grouping academically similar students allows for more appropriate advanced instruction, which matches the rapidly developing skills and capabilities of gifted students.

The power to meet the academic needs of the gifted student is in the hands of the school administrator. A quick look across any school will reveal more than half of the students identified as gifted are under achieving. The 1984 National Commission on Excellence in Education revealed half of the students identified as gifted failed to achieve a level which matched their abilities. That was the start of the unmasking of the achievement level of advanced learners. 25 years later, current research found that as high as 52 percent of gifted students in grades Kindergarten through twelfth grade are underachievers at a point in their education journey.[8] As expressed, there are no federal mandates in place to require the service to our gifted children. Parents and schools have the ability to research and offer the best acceleration options for their children.

The following are suggestions for adding learning capacity to the education of the gifted student from "20 Types of Acceleration" in the Acceleration Institute at the Belin-Blank Center:[9]

1. Early entrance into kindergarten targeting early readers.
2. First grade early admission.
3. Acceleration of grade levels: skipping a grade.
4. Continuous Progress: mastery of course content moves the student to the next level.
5. *Self-paced Instruction*: the student has control over all pacing decisions.
6. *Content-based Acceleration*: students enjoy classes with older peers.
7. Pre-testing students of all grade levels to gain information on placement in an advanced course above their grade level.
8. Clustering multi-aged gifted students into accelerated courses which move at a quicker pace.
9. Providing opportunities for students to test out of courses in a required course sequence. This allows the student to skip to the next course level.
10. Skipping a grade level. Research the social impact prior to making this choice.
11. Taking early college courses as part of their high school core and elective options.

12. Selecting Advanced Placement, International Baccalaureate or Cambridge courses for core and elective options.
13. Making accelerated online courses accessible through pre-approval, free technology and a supervised location on campus.
14. Making the school campus available to local colleges to offer evening courses for current students and area adults.
15. Conducting summer acceleration courses or camps.

The accessibility of acceleration options reflects a school leader's belief in serving all students at their learning level. This takes a flexible mindset with applicable knowledge of the school district, state and federal course requirements. If completed properly, the master schedule and campus options will align with the current student needs. The implementation of these initiatives may meet challenges from those who like the status quo. A student-centered school leader finds the solutions to prevail.

The Players in the Construction of the Master Schedule

The rationale behind the master schedule course content that benefits gifted students has been previously explored. The school leader is ready to put the pieces together with this critical student data as the foundation. There are experts in the school who are necessary in the building process for multiple reasons. These staff members will follow their transformational leader who values their input in making student-oriented decisions.

Who is at the table to assist the school leaders in building the master schedule?

The teacher leaders in the school have a pulse on the staff's attitudes and culture. In general, these teacher leaders are grade-team leaders in elementary schools and department leaders in secondary schools. Their inclusion in the building process offers the school leader a peak at the pulse of their areas of expertise. These teacher leaders are given an opportunity to be on the ground floor when building the master schedule.

Specialists in Exceptional Student Education, Gifted Education, and English Language Learners are also invited to participate and offer their opinions. Imagine a master schedule built with a school leader directing and listening to these knowledgeable student advocates. That students-first image is close to what the school leader will produce.

Most likely, an administrative trainee will be invited to the table. These are assistant or vice principals who are learning the process. This is part of the school leader's succession plan to generate a sustainable student-centered master building culture. By including a possible successor, the process will hold its validity for future school years. Understand that the data gathering, and course placement tasks associated with the building process are only half of the work to be completed. It is the affective or human side of the master schedule which requires a leader to skillfully lead people into making the best decisions for all students.

A minimum of school counselors and school secretaries are present at the table for multiple reasons. First, personal teacher information will be discussed. The teacher's abilities, future plans, past experiences, etc. are considered variables in making scheduling decisions. This information is fun fodder for the internal school grapevine. The minimum number of teacher leaders and teacher specialists are advised to keep the confidentiality of staff members or be removed from the process.

A truly student-centered master schedule is not necessarily counselor centered. The perfect counselor driven master schedule will place each student into a set schedule of grade level courses. Each individual student schedule would mirror the other. This method is not what is best for the student. In this case, it is left to the specialists to meet the students' needs through these set schedules. Student proficiency levels are secondary to grade levels or to the following of a course sequence. Graduating students is a counselor's primary concern.

> ***Teacher on the Master Schedule Team:*** *I have never worked with my administration on the master schedule before this. I can't believe we have to start so early. I was surprised at all the different variables we have to consider. I liked my team. We listened to each other and were not territorial. As the grade-level team leader, I had the chance to make some changes that will help our students next year. I was glad to be invited and listened to by my principal.*

Co-hort scheduling takes a considerable amount of resources to effectively schedule students into the same elective and core classes within one pathway. The most important resource to a counselor is their time. Placing students into a schedule driven by their pathway requires the finesse and time of a counselor. The benefits of a co-hort schedule is the clustering of like-minded students into one pathway. This places students together into their selected pathway of small learning communities. This model can be understood by comparing it to a large university's separation into colleges within their system. Pathway examples are career academies, programs of study, subject driven co-horts and gifted or another exceptionality co-horts.

The delegation of the master schedule to an assistant principal, school counselor, or other support person, gives that person the power in the school. The principalship or headmaster position comes with an ego-centric environment. It is easy to point a finger and the master schedule magically arrives on time and complete. If the leader only knows the basics and is not willing to take on the heavy lifting, they are not aware of the complexities of their school.

Ask the teachers who complete the master schedule. Their response is the name of the person who holds the power at the school. Conversely, the shrewd assistant principal or other person who is assigned this task can not only use it to learn how to run their own school but use it to lead the school's faculty and staff without the leader's input.

School and Class Schedules for Student-Centered Learning

The class schedule start and end times are frequently beyond the reach of the school leader to make changes. Many schools and school districts have set schedules for elementary, middle and high schools. For the most part these schedules are based on student transportation. The use of buses is more efficient and cost effective if the schedules are staggered with the starting and ending times of each level of school. Smaller school communities have more choices to adapt their school schedule to meet student needs.

The majority of schools have designated days for regular and special school days. Regular days follow a set pattern of opening and closing times. Special days are half or full school days designed to make time for conferences, teacher planning or professional development.

The scheduling of classes within the prescribed start and end times has higher potential to be influenced by the school leader. Elementary schools build their schedules to place students into grade levels and specials (electives). Teachers receive their required planning periods while their students are with their teachers of music, physical education, art or other designated electives. There is little room for adjustment in this prescribed class scheduling. Consequently, teacher assignment and gifted program implementation are even more important.

There are options for an elementary teacher to "roll up" or "loop" with their students to the next grade level. Depending on the quality and knowledge of the teacher, this is an extraordinary benefit to the gifted student. The teacher knows the student's acuity and abilities and can confidently advocate for their acceleration. This method enhances the education of the lower-level learner for the same reasons.

Secondary class schedules are varied and complex. Secondary schools may offer between six and eight classes. Below are a few middle and high school examples of student schedules for six classes:

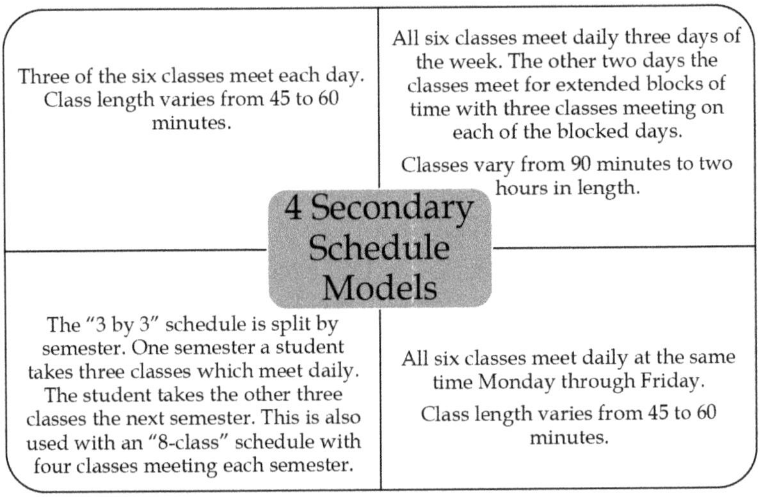

The best schedule for the student is dependent on the school leader's interpretation of the student's needs and their school budget. The more classes offered, the higher the price is to educate one student. There are positive and negative elements with each scheduling model that will directly affect students. It is dependent on the school leader to research their options carefully.

There is an abundance of schedules which include variables such as a constant period in the morning or at lunch time. The secondary Power Hour is a novel concept where students are assigned lunch for one half of the hour and the other half is their time to visit teachers, attend club meetings, remediate, or socialize.

The longer classes allow the teacher and the student time to explore their knowledge and collaborate with peers during project-based learning. The fewer classes scheduled in a school day, the more attention the course receives from every level of learner the night prior to the class.

Reading Discussion Activities

1. Research and write out the answers to the questions in the box at the beginning of the chapter.
2. Explain how your school meets the requirements to serve gifted children. Next, describe how the process can be improved. Be specific in each level of accommodations. Write these improvements as if funding or staffing was not an issue.
3. List the players and their assigned duties in the building of your school's master schedule with the advice from this chapter.

Chapter 8
The Master Schedule's Creation Calendar

The well-organized calendar that includes detailed steps in the creation of the master schedule is pivotal to its success. As with all large projects with many moving parts, time has the capacity to be a friend or an enemy. As discussed in previous sections, the school leader sets the precedent of authority early in the process.

The staff will be keenly aware that this leader has the final say on the master schedule and its building process. This authority structure will relieve the stress of some staff members. They want direction. They want their opinions considered. They want to know the master schedule will be completed on time.

The master schedule data spreadsheet

The master schedule's student-centered foundation is the data used to build each part. These data points are generalized as: district and federal policies, student course requests, teacher qualifications, staffing, facility needs, time, and the inclusion of staff to gain expert input and their support. We will explore the calendar with explanations for why each date is critical and how they relate to serving the advanced student.

Each school year starts with the return of an energized staff ready to welcome their students on their first day of school. The preparations include creating a welcoming environment for staff and students. This is when the school leader starts the next school year's master schedule. Yes, the master schedule for the *next school year* is in the processes of being built when the *previous year starts.* As odd as it may seem, the teachers, students and staff are quick to give their opinions on their preferences as they march confidently into their new school year.

Pay attention to the student responses, teacher comments and facility adaptation issues. Students from out of state or the country will arrive days prior to the opening of school. Their course selections were not considered in the building of the current year's schedule. Take notes on these opinions and observations and place them into the next school year's Master Schedule file.

As the first two months of school pass, there is a welcome rhythm which occurs on campus. The first term, generally a quarter, closes with the teachers and students set in a predictable pattern of expectations of each other. At the conclusion of the first grading period is a natural time to start next year's master schedule's processes. The staff and students have the confidence to continue through a predictable current school year while gently receiving nudges from their administration on preparation for the next year.

Teacher preference survey

The first task is to **survey current teachers** on their preferences for the next school year. This form is sent to teachers through their email around the start of the third month of the current school year, after the first quarter or grading period. This activity builds school culture. This process produces trust between each teacher and their supervisor. See a sample survey in *Appendix C.*

It is not recommended for the teachers to give their team leaders or department leaders their preferences. They may not want the teacher leaders to know their preferences. These requests have the capacity to be politically charged. Especially, if the teacher indicates they are not happy with their teacher-leader, desire different courses, or want to take their position. This method presents the opportunity for the school leader to be informed that the teacher may not be returning the next school year. This information is critical in staffing and the earlier it is known, the better for the future students in the class.

> ***Middle School National Board-Certified Teacher:*** *This is my third school. I've taught all levels of English from 6th to 12th grade in three schools. I know how to teach every kind of student. I left my other schools because I did not agree with the administration on how to teach kids. Today, I found out my principal wants to know what I want to teach. She is meeting with each teacher, alone, to find out what they want. I sincerely appreciate the time this will take. I think I am going to stay at this school for a while.*

Conversely, the teacher may tell the teacher-leader information not given to the school administration. This situation is addressed in the building of the teams or departments in a later section. The confidential **Teacher Preference Survey** *(Appendix C)* is a simple one-page document submitted in hardcopy or through email. Teachers include their credentials, including certifications or endorsements in progress and will be completed by the next school year. Remember, one of the school leader's required documents to have on hand is the spreadsheet of all their staff's credentials.

Furthermore, this information allows the school leader to grant the preferences of good teachers as a reward for their positive work with students. Or, the school leader may use these preferences to help a less effective teacher find another assignment. Taking note on the identification of teachers who are effective with special need students (gifted students, math remediation, second language learners, etc.) leads the way to meeting the needs of more students. For example, a teacher with a high ability in working with gifted students, may indicate her preference is to follow a unique model to provide support.

School leaders will learn from their expertise how to better serve these students. Include a preference on room assignment or planning time. These forms are put aside or entered into a confidential spreadsheet for later reference in the master schedule building process.

Individualized student registration sheets

The development of the next school year's student registration sheets starts in October of the current school year. The previous section outlines, in detail, the importance of creating a unique registration sheet for each school year. By starting in October, the school leader has the opportunity to review the teacher preferences, research course options outside of current offerings, predict needed remediation courses from the current year's first quarter data and review the current year's success in meeting specialized student needs.

The new school year will have different student data sets to consider. This is the rationale behind building registration options which are unique for each school year. It takes time for the registration staff to enter the data required to build each student's individualized registration sheet. The deadline for their creation is the week after the first semester grades are posted. This timeline gives the data entry staff time to enter the grades (passing or failing) into the student's data set which will reflect their course needs on their individualized registration sheet.

The student is the reader of their individualized student registration sheets. Each sheet is built with their frame of reference in mind. The registration process is started and completed in the first month following the close of the first term or semester. It is common that students enjoy a "next year" mindset after the winter break. All students receive their individualized registration sheets a week prior to their required submission *(Appendix B.1 & B.2).*

Each school will appreciate a different process in distributing the registration materials. This is an exciting time for students. Make it fun for them! As expressed in the previous section, a Registration Fair is recommended but not essential. The important factors in determining the distribution process is the time and staff access needed to make good course selections and time for parental input.

Teacher leaders gain ownership through the master schedule building process

The student registration data and the teacher preference survey are submitted and recorded into spreadsheets for easy access. The data is both aggregated and disaggregated. Now is the time to start partnering the classes, teachers and time schedule (class periods, class blocks, specials, etc.).

The master schedule building team receives the spreadsheets at different times and levels. It is advisable to give the elementary team leader or the secondary department leader this data. Remember, they are on the school leader's master schedule building team. This practice gives these teacher-leaders input and ownership of the process. It is rare that they will refuse participation in this activity. It is their choice to include the members on their team or in their departments. However, it is critical they keep the confidence of the students, teachers and administrators in any discussions with staff outside the master schedule building team.

The school leader explains to these delegated teacher leaders that their work is a draft. Their input is valuable and critical to the process as they are the subject or grade level expert. The school leader has the final decision on the master schedule. Teacher leaders have a greater ability to learn important information from their teachers.

These cohesive teams and departments are mini families. The trusted teacher leader may learn one of their teachers is leaving the school, having a baby, wanting another teacher's room or assignment, etc. This is an additional opportunity for the school leader to find out if a teacher is leaving or staying prior to finalizing the next school year's master schedule.

Let's look at the creation life cycle of the master schedule:

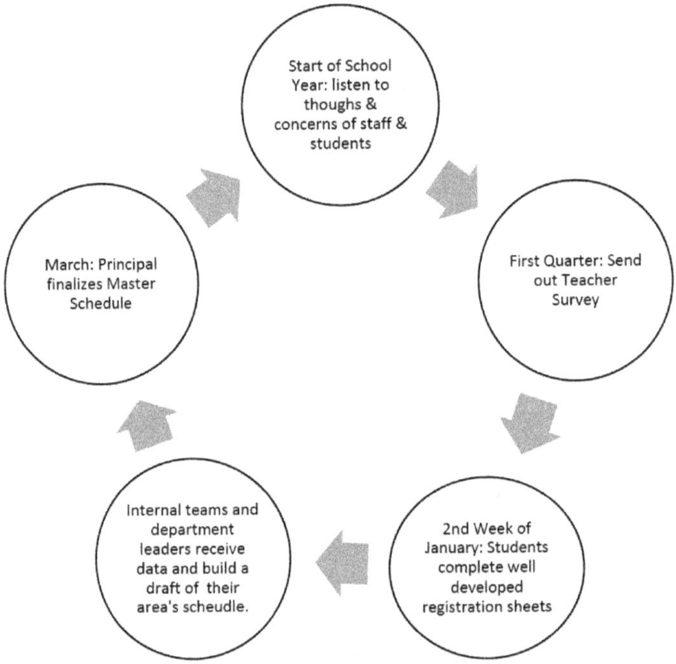

School leader builds the master schedule

At this point in February, the school leader has critical information to the building of their next year's master schedule. They have at hand: student data, teacher preferences and the departmental and team recommendations for scheduling. Now is the time to close the door and get to work. The amount of time needed for this process is dependent on the leader's efficiency and ability to create a final product. It is recommended that this time is protected from other duties or interruptions. The size of the school and the implementation of new programs has an effect on timing.

Models for building a master schedule that include the data are color coded wall boards, extensive spreadsheets and chart paper. Regardless of the preferred model, this information is highly sought after by all staff. If a staff member reports what they see on a board, drama will follow. Keep the processing of the master schedule private until the draft is ready for the master schedule building team.

The presentation of the first master schedule draft to the team

By the first week of March, the master schedule draft has been built by the school leader. There is a brief time prior to bringing in the master schedule team to review the draft that the school leaders need to move a few mountains. This is when the school leaders pull in teachers to negotiate assignment changes, recruit staff, and seek funding for future programs, and communicate with supervisors their plans for change.

The amount of time allotted for this important part of building the master schedule relies on the school leader's need to solidify their changes. The naysayers who disagree with the school leader's changes will know the research has been completed and the initiatives are in place for the new year. The work completed in this critical time period communicates to the master schedule building team that the school leader is in charge and these student-centered initiatives are in place.

The draft is then presented to the master schedule building team for their input. Set aside a large meeting area that is somewhat soundproof. Snacks and lunch are always appreciated. Provide substitutes for teachers. It is not recommended to fit in this process after school or on a weekend. The leader wants the team to feel comfortable and safe in sharing opinions.

The teacher leaders are present and negotiate the differences between their submitted draft and the school leader's draft. Listening to the staff is critical in developing a viable schedule. Their expertise gives the school leader options for changes.

Discussions include the questions and concerns of the school counselor. Remember, their priority is to graduate students and their most valuable asset is time. Their input is highly valuable and will provide the leader with information on how scheduling the students will be impacted by the course offerings and their location in the schedule.

This process takes several sessions. Monitor and remind the team their confidence is critical. These are jury rules. Do not discuss the building of the master schedule outside the team's room.

Master schedule draft is publicized to all staff

Revealing the contents of the next year's master schedule is conducted differently dependent on the school's culture. "The reveal" can be a celebration. A faculty meeting reveal is a less personal method. It is preferred to work with individual teams or departments for the reveal. The department or team leaders who served on the master schedule building team are essential in the reveal process.

It is critical to let all staff members know this is a tentative schedule. Changes occur with student enrollment and staff changes. This timing gives the school leader several weeks to hold individual teacher meetings to discuss their preferences for a change.

Another school culture building opportunity for school leaders is to give each teacher a final printed tentative schedule prior to their departure for the summer break. This can be completed individually by visiting the teacher's classroom during their planning or another convenient time for them. This is an opportunity to celebrate the teacher with encouragement in preparation for the next school year.

This is yet another opportunity for a teacher to communicate their intentions to return the next school year. Plus, teachers will use this information to collaborate with peers and prepare next year's their lessons. It's a win-win for the students and their teachers. This personal touch is appreciated by staff. Any changes to these tentative schedules are communicated immediately during the summer months prior to the teacher's return for the new school year.

Master Schedule Creation Timeline

Time Period	Activity
Start of current school year	Notes from Staff and Students
End of first quarter	Teacher Preference Survey
October, November	Student Registration sheets developed
2nd week of January	Student Registration sheets distributed. Grades for first term are in. Students have a "next year" mindset. Google docs, hard copies, Rising student procedures

February – first two weeks	Team and department leaders receive data to build their area's schedule
February – last two weeks	The board – large format building area – building is drafted. Two weeks to build – keeps priorities of school leader's time sacred for all staff and districts to know
March: week 1	School leader pulls in teachers, negotiates, recruits, seeks funding
March: week 2	Include counselors. Variable with spring breaks
March: week 3	MS is finalized
April	The reveal
May: week 1	Teachers receive their tentative schedules for the next school year
From June to start of school	Training, collaboration teams, etc.

The school leader has more authority then they realize over how their school's master schedule affects their school's culture. By actively taking responsibility for the process the leader positively impacts all students. A student-centered master schedule will offer the necessary and best programs for special student populations.

Gifted students will thrive in a student-centered schedule that is built for their needs and with consideration of their unique requests. The leader's knowledge of district, state and federal laws will allow them to create innovative programs specific to their student population. Quality staffing, consistent accountability structures and a quest for a positive school culture will guide the leader of the master scheduling team.

Purposefully building a school's master schedule to meet the needs of special student populations, especially gifted students, are showcased with proven examples. It is pivotal to the success of gifted secondary students to build a school's master schedule which facilitates the advanced learner.

Diverse populations have unique curricular needs. These needs are addressed through co-hort scheduling and purposefully aligning programs to meet the gifted student's interests. The savvy administrator builds accelerated courses to both group and distribute their high-level learners.

Reading Discussion Activities

1. Build your school's Master Schedule Data Spreadsheet as described This will start as a shell. Fill in your current knowledge.
2. Explain how you will communicate with the staff and the steps to implement the Teacher Preference Survey. Next, determine how you will use the survey data.
3. Using the Master Schedule Timeline chart at the end of the chapter, fill in the dates, tasks and responsible staff in additional columns.

Chapter 9
Hiring and Training Advocates for All Advanced Learners

Hire staff that "get" students. School leaders recognize a student's exceptionality in aptitude and achievement requires diverse teaching strategies. Learning takes place with appropriately differentiated lessons designed to stretch students to their full learning potential. This definition of a gifted student is part of the staff hiring section as a reminder of the end game: The type of lesson directly correlates to the development of a gifted child's full learning potential.

> ***7th Grade Gifted Student:** I love going to Ms. Jackson's class. She really gets me. Then, when I go to science, Mr. Walsh thinks I am a troublemaker. I love science and I know so much more about it than he does. Why doesn't he let me talk? It's just weird how some teachers get me, and others don't. I hope 8th grade will be better. I wish the teachers would get together and talk about how to teach kids like me.*

Creating a supportive gifted culture starts with hiring school staff who recognize the unique needs of the gifted student. What are the attributes of a teacher who meets the needs of a student who requires acceleration? These traits are found in the teacher who has an instinct in recognizing the needs of any child.

The school leader is ultimately responsible for how and what teachers present in the classroom. It is essential for the hiring authority to develop the ability to gauge a teacher's aptitude for meeting the academic needs of all students during the hiring process.

The ability to differentiate what makes a highly effective teacher of the gifted cannot be identified by age, gender, university attended or the type of teaching credentials. A champion gifted teacher brings out the best in their students. Their classroom is open to new ideas, a safe place to fail, collaborative, organized, predictable, and often noisy. It is left to the school leader to discover if a teacher candidate has this potential.

Recognize a good teacher of gifted students during the hiring interview

The interview process can be refined to include a few additional questions that reveal the belief system of the teacher-candidate. Veteran teachers carry with them examples of past experiences and multiple recommendations regarding their effective teaching practices. However, the conversation must reveal their specific gifted teaching knowledge. Key phrases and attitudes are telling in their interview responses. The less experienced candidates are asked questions to discern their overall attitude in creating a positive learning environment for all levels of learners and how the advanced learner fits into these expectations.

The hiring of support personnel as a positive part of a gifted culture follows similar practices in the discovery of their true opinions of what is best for the advanced learner. For example, school counselors commonly have a service mindset. They will clarify their flexibility, acute knowledge of the gifted student's idiosyncrasies, availability for confidential emotional support and parent advocacy, among other strengths.

The school leader is searching for qualified teachers who are flexible in their teaching assignments. As the builder of the master schedule, the school leader includes prized teachers who hold multiple subject and grade level credentials. Plus, teachers are invaluable who hold specialty credentials in gifted, second language learners and special education. Adding to accelerated options, the teacher with a master's degree has the potential of teaching dual enrollment, or early college courses.

❑❑❑

These five interview questions are in addition to the standard hiring questions. Each question provides the candidate with an opportunity to showcase their knowledge of advanced learners.

1. Give a specific example of a lesson where you differentiated your instruction techniques to challenge students. (*Candidates will reveal the level of their understanding of differentiation and how it applies to acceleration.)*

2. Describe what it means to be gifted. *(This open question gives the candidate room to use their own words to reveal their attitude toward gifted students.)*

3. What are your expectations for individual support in a classroom where there may be a sense of equality of knowledge or understanding between you and your students? (*The gifted student may know more than their teacher on some subjects. How will the teacher respond to their superior knowledge?)*

4. Give an example of how you meet the social and emotional needs of the advanced learner. (*This question reveals the teacher's holistic knowledge of the gifted child.)*

5. What techniques do you utilize to guide your students in the reflection of their own understanding? Give an example. (*The reflective practice leads the gifted student into a deeper understanding of what they think and why they think it.)*

Unique Teacher Training for the Purposeful Support of Gifted Students

"The best teacher is the one who never forgets what it is like to be a student. The best administrator is the one who never forgets what it is like to be a teacher."

Neila A. Connors [1]

Leading a school with an ability to put oneself into the shoes of teachers is pivotal in knowing how to serve an instructional staff. The respect for the expertise of teachers is communicated through every type of leader's interaction. An astute school leader embeds positive energy into every communication and action with their teachers.

Professional development can be just another required training that takes time away from what teachers need to do. With a few positive shifts in how trainings are conducted, a teacher may actually look forward to meeting with colleagues and learning new skills. It is the school leader's goal to receive positive comments about the relevancy of the training from honest teachers.

To begin, bury the myth that gifted students are just fine in regular classrooms with a few extra assignments. Teachers attempt to challenge all students. Through no fault of their own, they are frequently unacquainted with the needs of gifted children and do not know how to best serve them in the classroom.

The Fordham Institute found in a national study that 58% of teachers received no professional development that focused on teaching academically advanced students in the past few years. Additionally, 73% of teachers reported that that "too often, the brightest students are bored and underchallenged in school – we are not giving them a sufficient chance to thrive." This report confirms what many students and their parents have claimed: not all teachers are able to recognize and support advanced learners.[2]

The school leader communicates the message that "gifted students are important" by providing teacher training on how to meet the academic and social needs of advanced learners. Teachers will purposefully plan instruction when they know this is important to their administration. There is minimal expense for a teacher to adapt their current instructional strategies and modify their curriculum.

The professional development of teachers must be relevant to be effective. The school leader needs data that reveal the level of need and what type of professional development is required to impact the instruction of gifted students. It is a waste of time to assume what an instructional staff needs. They may have a deep understanding of how to serve gifted students and simply need resources to conduct their lessons.

The effective school leader knows the teacher's opinions on Gifted Education

Take the temperature of the teachers in the school. What is their opinion of the gifted student? Do they want to have a deeper understanding of how to teach advanced learners?

Creating a short survey to distribute to current staff delivers the temperature of the school's gifted culture. A short 10 to 15 item survey conducted anonymously with direct questions gives an administrator a place to start with their professional development. In most schools, teachers are forthright about their opinions on teaching and learning. If a trusted school leader wants a straight answer on what and how learning is occurring in their school: just ask a teacher.

Sample Questions for an Administrative Survey for Staff to Assess the Gifted School Climate

1. Are all gifted students in our school served with what they need to excel?
2. Are linguistically diverse gifted students served with the same time and support as others?
3. Are students with culturally diverse backgrounds served appropriately?
4. Do regular education teachers recognize the expected outcomes of the gifted program?
5. Do gifted education teachers comprehend the purpose of the school's gifted program?
6. Is accelerated curriculum available to teachers of gifted students?
7. What are the needs of teachers with gifted students?
8. Are all teachers provided professional development in gifted instruction?
9. Are all teachers given training in differentiated instruction?
10. Do all teachers have access to PD in addressing the needs of diverse populations?

Adapted from: Naglieri et al., (2008) *Helping All Gifted Children Learn: A Teachers Guide to Using the NNAT2.*

The results of the survey are in and the school leader and their assistants are ready to start training the teachers. Stick to the data produced by the survey. It is deplorable to give a survey to appease the teacher into thinking their opinion matters, then go through with the training planned prior to the gathering of survey data. Remember, all communication from the school leader either builds up or breaks down trust.

Targeted and Relevant Professional Development through Master Teachers

Creating effective training does not require a full school overall. There are people in place who are skilled in presenting information and knowledgeable about the targeted subjects. Gently tweak what is in place for a more effective impact on the classroom.

Implementing small steps at a time leads to high-performing training systems. These incremental improvements are studied and kept in the system when effective and discarded when they fail. This pragmatic approach to revamping a school's professional development is built for sustainability.

Rebrand the expert presenters. The new professional "learning leaders" are the common peer "teacher leaders" and trained along with other school leaders in the presentation content. These master practitioners come in pairs or more. Personalities are mixed up by having more than one learning leader per subject. The teachers are a part of the school's faculty and carry with them a reputation for highly effective gifted student instruction (or other subject). This is a low-cost tweak to a school's professional development system because the learning leaders are already on the faculty.

How are master practitioners in gifted education selected from a staff of knowledgeable teachers? First, consider their level of knowledge. Second, consider their relationship with the staff. Are there opinions respected? Do they use encouraging communication skills? Let the chosen staff know that the master practitioner role is not just another duty. Find something to take off their plate as an incentive to join the professional development team.

Elementary Teacher: *My Gifted Learning Leader partners are all different. Peggy is such a curmudgeon. But, boy does she know a lot about gifted. When we are building our presentations, she has so much valuable input. I like to talk on stage. I'm a natural entertainer. So, she gladly sits and watches while I present our ideas. Of course, I receive her critical analysis of my performance after our presentation. I would not have it any other way.*

It is a rare situation when the school leader is the ultimate school authority on gifted education or any specialty other than their current position or past teaching assignment. So, let the master practitioners develop the training. Their objectives will be student-centered. Their pedagogical suggestions come directly from their professional experiences. Let them be in charge of how and what to present.

Interestingly, by giving the teachers the authority to train their peers, the school's past professional develop practices will disappear. Teachers can be highly judgmental on how they have been trained in the past. Of course, they are critics, this is their chosen profession. Good teachers are great at teaching. And, even mediocre teachers have some honed skills in presenting. School leaders should watch and learn from their example.

The content of the gifted education professional development is based on the student's needs as determined by the master practitioners. They have the option of surveying the staff or students to gather data prior to starting to build their training content. Encourage the survey. It may be enlightening on where the student needs originate.

"Let's talk about how Johnny learns."
"This method works for Sarah."

The content of the professional development sessions directed at meeting the needs of gifted students can be anecdotal. In the inter-school environment, using student names is acceptable because of the faculty's experience with the specific gifted student. Teachers will have a deep personal experience in teaching the named student. This method is highly effective as the teachers can relate and learn immediately applicable strategies for that student and future gifted students. This anecdotal method is not acceptable outside of the school family. As a caveat, refer to named students as if their parents (or lawyers) are sitting in the back of the room.

Watch how the master practitioners use collaboration as a teaching tool for their peers. They understand they may be experts in gifted education, but they are not an expert in teaching mathematics, physics, physical education, etc. By presenting a strategy and letting the subject level or grade level teachers discuss its implementation, great learning takes place. The school leader will learn from these collaborative groups as they report-out the results of their discussion.

When one or more teachers are gathered without school management present, there will be both negative and positive reflections passionately and clearly voiced to the group (especially if it is at the end of a school day). Understand that by placing peer trainers in front of other teachers, a safe environment for open off-topic discussions occurs. The school leader has a choice to be present for these open discussions. A belief in the ability of the master practitioners to present their content and entertain off-topic discussions induces even more trust in their leadership and that of their peer teachers. Of course, it is always best for school leaders to participate in professional development with their teachers. However, know when to be absent and allow teachers to talk among themselves. Conversely, know when to stay to learn and monitor discussions.

Unique Challenges in Gifted Education Professional Development

Many gifted students have a unique ability to be one step ahead of their teachers in both academics and behavior. Some students use this power for good, others for not so good. Essential professional development directed at how to inspire learning in an advanced student is more than acquiring pedagogical structures.

A high IQ in an adolescent who does not respect or like their teacher is a recipe for a long frustrating school year for both the student and the teacher. Many well-meaning teachers have thrown in the towel after a precocious student learned how to repeatedly push their buttons. This is a situation that does not require behavior discipline from the teacher or administration. It requires fundamental professional development from a master practitioner in gifted education.

The school leader has an understanding of the professional development content and can recognize its application in the classroom. Teachers are asked to invite the administrators and master practitioners into their classroom to see evidence of their training in action.

These classroom visitations can proceed by invitation or by drop-in. This active leadership presence increases the self-efficacy of the teacher as they confidently showcase their talents. Additionally, teachers are asked to invite their school leaders and peer teachers into their classrooms to view projects and interesting student activities.

Teacher-mentors are provided for struggling teachers or to teachers who request additional classroom support for their gifted students. The learning leaders develop a level of trust with their peers through their encouraging and nurturing attention. This mutual respect has the capacity to substantially change a school culture and raise the learning levels of all students.

Three Examples of Effective Gifted Education Professional Development Topics

While earning their teaching credential, budding teachers are exposed to a variety of instructional techniques through their university or employee onboarding process. An emphasis is often placed on how to work with diverse learning populations with much of their specialized training centered around the needs of students who qualify for special education services. Yet most classrooms are filled with all levels of learners. Federal law requires that instructional and behavioral support is provided for students struggling to learn at their grade level. Exceptional learning needs are on both ends of the spectrum.

School administrators are aware teachers are not provided with formalized training on giftedness. Understanding the gifted student's exceptional needs is the first step for a school leader and their teachers to provide a positive and appropriate learning environment. The master practitioners or current teachers with professional experience in successfully teaching gifted students are an administrator's greatest resource. These teachers frequently have a passionate heart for their advanced students and are willing to help them by providing professional development to their peers.

All students deserve to experience academic challenges. If a school leader is meeting the requirement for gifted instruction by clustering advanced learners in regular classrooms, then it is even more critical for the teachers to be well trained in gifted educational strategies.

This training will enable teachers to understand giftedness and how to identify and appropriately serve their needs. Consider the research on how to effectively meet the academic and social-emotional needs of gifted children through enhanced and informed instruction. An important pre-professional development session is recommended to explore gifted social emotional characteristics as well as highlight asynchronistic developments, over excitability, perfectionism and anxiety. These may be unfamiliar concepts to some teachers.

Below are three methods of teaching as they relate to the instruction of gifted students. The first, holistic thinking, is an open-idea method which allows the student to explore a self-directed learning style. The second, competency-based learning, allows the gifted student the freedom to jump forward to their personal level of learning. The third, Curriculum Compacting, presents the gifted student with modified content which moves them forward to topics yet to be discovered.

1. Holistic Thinking Within the Content Area

A teacher who has the ability to teach with holistic teaching methods organically meets the intellectual needs of the gifted student. The domains of intellect, emotion, intuition and imagination reside within these lessons. The student is called upon to locate a nucleus of an idea and expand on it through an outreaching web of discovery, experimentation and research.

A classroom walkthrough during this discovery phase of holistic learning looks and sounds different than a traditional classroom. Most teachers are taught to teach with a predetermined sequence of presented content. After the majority of the class masters this content, the teacher moves to the next step in the sequence.

Holistic learning looks for mastery within the content, yet not necessarily in a sequence. A group of children working on discovering the solution to a math problem may look odd to a passing administrator. Their dialogue is expressive as they call upon previously learned material while utilizing inference to determine the solution. This is frequently a loud process. Silent children working independently at their desks in a neat row is not occurring.

A teacher with an open mind and a diverse teaching tool kit can become skilled at using holistic learning. This varied instructional approach generates trust between the teacher and the student. They can sense the teacher's interest in their individual differences and how they learn. This trust allows the student to take academic risks in exploring innovative ideas and taking on difficult problems.

The inclusion of holistic learning is critical in a school's basket of required teacher training. Gifted students frequently have a unique perspective on learning due to their acute ability to infer relationships between and within concepts. A safe classroom to a gifted child is defined as an accepting environment to ask questions, challenge ideas, and accelerate their own abilities through challenging peer interactions. The time and funds spent on teaching the practice of holistic instruction and learning will exponentially increase learning.[3]

2. The gifted students thrive in a classroom of competency-based learning

This method of instruction is in direct contrast to clustering students by age in the current grade leveling system. Obviously, students of the same age learn differently. That is a content-driven model of instruction as opposed to a student-driven model. In the past, the time spent on course content was part of a predetermined course mapping with a scope and sequence. The teacher led all students through the content to a scheduled assessment, then moved on to the next section of content presented with the same calendar structure.

Competency-based education starts with what the student knows and moves forward to what they do not know. Once the content is mastered, the student moves to the next section, and so on. The movement to the next content is based on competence not the calendar.

This method calls for an individualized learning process. The seat time for each part of the course content is different for each child. Furthermore, the teacher may determine that the previous standard of mastery at achieving a 60% is not acceptable.

The competency-based classroom looks different. There are mixed ages of students learning at different rates. Differentiated instruction is used to enhance the learning of all students at their own level. Students advance at their own pace while experiencing how mastering pushes everyone to a higher standard. The status quo is no longer acceptable as mastery as students strive toward the metric of mastery determined by the teacher. Earning an 80% is a common expectation for mastery in competency-based instruction.

3. The joy of curriculum compacting to enhance gifted learning

The grade level of the gifted student rarely reflects their understanding of the academic content assigned to that grade. This method of differentiated instruction evaluates the prior knowledge of the individual student and condenses the related course content. The teacher streamlines the regular curriculum to reduce repetition of previously mastered course content.

The compacting of what students already know provides class time for enrichment beyond the basic content. Similar to competency-based learning, the acceleration is practiced by assessing the prior knowledge of the individual student. This method includes previously mastered content, but in a condensed delivery.

Teachers who utilize Curriculum Compacting determine their unit or lesson goals, assess students for prior knowledge, then write their lessons to differentiate instruction. Positive outcomes of this method are in the opportunities to provide enrichment opportunities. Done properly, teachers can eliminate a high percentage of curriculum without negatively impacting test scores. Professional development is important to train teachers in how to modify instruction and find related replacement activities for enrichment.[4]

Reading Discussion Activities

1. Review the contents of the *Administrative Climate Survey* at the beginning of the chapter. Add 5 questions directly related to your school. Discuss the plan for confidential distribution.
2. List 5 areas of gifted education professional development needed by your school's staff. Next to each item, list the name of the master-teacher who has the experience and ability to provide training in these areas.
3. Brainstorm how your administrative team and master teachers can encourage all teachers to embed the three teaching methods in classes for all levels of learners in your school.

Chapter 10
Navigating Barriers to Promote the Success of Innovative Gifted Education Practices

Why do you want to help gifted students? They are going to graduate. Why spend your scarce funds to help the smart kids?

Principal speaking to a *school district supervisor*:

Hi, I need "*any named resource*" to support my gifted student population.

But wait, you can't do that.

Do what?

Give so much assistance to gifted kids.

Why not? My gifted students need this. I have data to prove it will work.

There are too many other students who need this resource.

Really? I need to serve all my students and my gifted students have obvious needs that my school is not meeting.

Well then, it's on you to find the resources.

OK...watch me take care of my students as I promised.

Consider the training and formal education received in preparation for taking the prized school leader position. There were graduate classes in positive and effective instructional leadership, education law, finance management, school-based data analysis, and general leadership practices. The core of each class and the localized leadership training involved placing the students as a priority. This is the promise made when accepting a position to lead a school of any level.

The school leader is observant and notices their advanced students are not learning at the top of their academic ability. With further investigation into the school data and casual inquiries to teachers, parents and students, the leader determines that changes need to occur to meet the needs of the school's gifted student population.

It is important to note in this section, that the school leader is commonly paid the same salary whether or not the students identified as gifted are adequately served in the school. It takes a passionately motivated leader to step out and do what is right by all students in the building. Conversely, it is common for a school administrator to be given additional resources or even displaced if the low-level learner data decreases while on their watch.

Middle School Principal: *As the principal of a choice magnet middle school, I visited one of our elementary feeder schools to "recruit" gifted students to my school which accepts all levels of learners yet accelerates students at a more rapid level than the surrounding non-choice schools. I was charged with increasing my underrepresented student population.*

As one of my strategies, I visited my feeder elementary schools to recruit in their 8th grade classes. A young man sat in the front of the class during my presentation. He was engaged and flung his arm up enthusiastically to answer and ask questions. As I left, I asked the school counselor and parent advocate to tell me about the young man. He seemed a natural fit for my school. They informed me that he could not enter my advanced school because he had an SLD (Specific Learning Disability). I asked the nature of his SLD. They indicated he recently arrived from Haiti and was learning English. I immediately responded that he was an ELL (English Language Learner), not SLD and I wanted him in my school.

His non-English speaking parents did not have the knowledge to advocate for him. I knew right away they had misdiagnosed a gifted child.

With this understanding, we can proceed to the revelations of barriers erected to slow down the process of meeting the needs of the high achieving student. The solutions demand a resilient leader with a laser focus on serving students. This is not for the leader who delegates authority to meet student needs, accepts the status quo, or is content to stay off the radar of supervisors.

The school leader overcomes the first barrier and moves to the second and third to serve the advanced learners in their school:

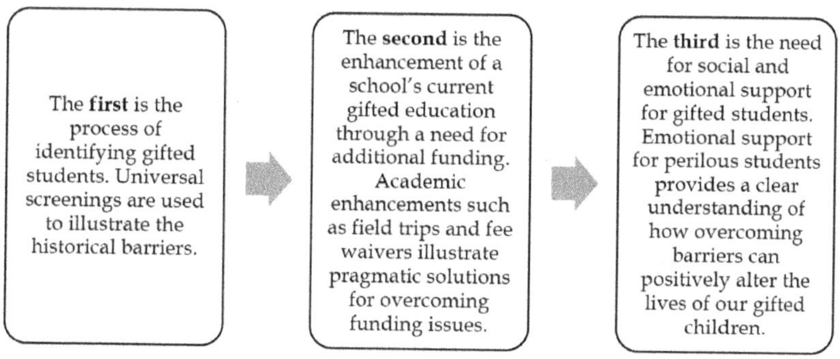

To facilitate an understanding of how to overcome barriers, leadership situations are divided into three unique categories of initiatives to serve students identified as gifted.

Why can't I screen all my students for gifted? We are missing students with the referral system.

To start, there is a longstanding understanding that gifted education has an underrepresentation of minorities and economically challenged groups. It can be assumed that the identification process may preclude these students from assessments. Elementary gatekeepers are teacher and parent referrals. Assessments are rarely given in the secondary years and when they occur, they are commonly for individual students requested through parent or teacher referrals.

Universal screening solves the problem of leaving out qualified students. The systematic failure of using referrals is repeated each school year. Yet, it is known that universal screening increases the representation of low-income and minority gifted students.

Ask the gifted assessment experts in your school about the details of the screening process. Listen for windows of opportunity to make changes. Listen for the barriers (funding, staff, rules, etc.). Do not accept an explanation which includes "that is how we have always done it" or "that is a district expectation, not a law." Learn the legal and state statute parameters for assessing gifted students. These are the legitimate boundaries. Any barrier set outside these boundaries is ripe for breaking down.

Determine exactly what is needed to successfully carry out this universal screening initiative. This includes funding, staff, facilities, procedures for parent permissions, etc. Take a clear look at the school resources by turning over "rocks." It is amazing how resources hide within the inner workings of a school. This is one more reason for the school leader to build the master schedule and be an active participant, if not the leader, in all areas of budget dissemination.

Next, write out exactly what the universal screening initiative will require. Include required staff, number of assessments, time, facility requirements, parent permissions, etc. Work with school-based or itinerate gifted experts to develop this plan. Every step and resources are on paper.

Establish a procedure and start the implementation with procuring the evaluative instruments. At the same time the gifted support staff is determine which students are already identified as gifted and who receives the screening. Parent permission slips are distributed. The screening materials may be in the school or available from other schools or the school district. Interestingly, once the grapevine of gifted support persons learns about the school's universal screening needs, the instruments start appearing. These student advocates help turn over the "rocks" at other schools to find what is needed.

Supervisors will learn about the initiative and want more information on the shift in the status quo. Express a passionate data-based reason for universal screening and what is needed to proceed. Any barriers can be toppled with the school leader's knowledge of state statutes and how the current system is built for the convenience of adults and not students.

Secondary school leaders may include that the exclusive second grade district screening is missing a plethora of secondary students. Past secondary screenings in the schools have revealed the identification of a high percentage of gifted students who have not been served because they were not tested in second grade or missed other opportunities. This, in a nutshell, is educational malpractice.

Gauge the supervisor's response by what it will take to serve the non-identified gifted student's needs. Know who is in charge. Do not take a "no" from a person who cannot give a "yes." (Oprah Winfrey) This is when the school leader explains exactly what is needed and why. This transparency reveals the student-centered reasons. Remember, the non-identified gifted students in the school are waiting for their champion to succeed.

Gather the troops. Make the initiative public to parents, school staff and school district allies. A supportive parent works to ensure the needs of their child are met as well as the needs of other children in their community. Parent groups are one of the most powerful entities in a school. No school district office wants to be confronted by parents. This leads to big issues that have the potential to explode on social media and the evening news. Publicize the results of your initial testing. It is difficult to pull the rug out from under a publicly supported student-centered initiative.

Observations by Nate's Gifted Support Teacher following his identification during a universal screening: *Nate gets lost in his world of music. He has extraordinary leadership skills. His parents almost removed him from his rigorous academic schedule. They saw a difference after receiving resources after Nate's identification as gifted. We focused on accountability. This Worked. A new support system helped Nate with time-management skills. He started turning in the work he completed. The result was a more relaxed and happier student with higher grades. The stress was off of him because his work no longer overwhelms him. As the gifted support teacher, I enjoy frequent contact with the parents.*

The school is increasing their gifted population. This means more funds are needed to purchase assessments, support staff, professional development and professional evaluators. Consider the following funding sources: Internal budgets (scan those spreadsheets for possible reallocations of funds), state allocated gifted education funds sent to districts (a search will reveal how much is allocated and where it is spent), apply for grants, reach out for business partner and parent donations (sponsor a child…). A school administrator with a strong and knowledgeable student focus and a servant-leader mindset for gifted students will succeed in acquiring resources for their school.

My gifted students need relevant experiences in their post-secondary options

My gifted students need relevant experiences in their post-secondary options to make good decisions and they can't afford the preparations needed to enter college.

As stated, the high achieving student is one of the most valuable resources in the nation. The children who have high achievement capability in areas such as intellectual, creative, artistic, leadership, or in specific academic fields require encouragement and services from their school. Without these supports, their giftedness will not reach full potential and bloom into a high achieving adult who is a great societal asset.

The family of a gifted student should not be responsible for providing information on the vast opportunities after high school. Of course, there are many parents who dive in and are an active part of the post-secondary academic process. As student numbers swell, the students identified as gifted are increasingly diverse in their ancestry and income. A school leader can make a lifelong difference in a child's life by providing post-secondary experiences before they graduate.

These services are directly related to making a choice of where to go and what to study after high school. A first-generation college or high school graduate may not have an in-home advocate who is knowledgeable about their opportunities. By embedding experiences into the secondary school years, each child is provided opportunities to explore their numerous options.

The structure of this initiative has a different level of experience for each grade level. For example, *freshmen* attend school assemblies presented by local, state and out-of-state education institutions; *sophomores* use school buses to travel to the local colleges for outstanding and informative presentations; *juniors* are bused to state and private universities; *seniors* are given a geographically specific out-of-state charter bus tour of select universities early in their senior year.

> ***10th Grade Gifted Student during a bus tour of local colleges:*** *I am not sure what I want to take in college. The school we visited was beautiful. Three of my friends want to go there. My parents did not go to college. They both work and could not take me to learn more about the schools. They want me to go to college close to home. I don't know what I'll do, I am just glad they are encouraging me to go.*

The information and experiences are priceless. They set a foundation for the student's goals and dreams. Additionally, the students may need funds to cover costs for college applications and required testing. These university exploration costs are an important resource for the students identified as gifted.

The barrier in providing these resources are costs and permissions to travel. School fund raising efforts are similar to the first barrier scenario. Look for funds in the internal budget, district offerings, grants, parent and business donations. The federal title 1 funds can be used for these efforts. The sponsoring of students is an effective fundraiser by parents, staff and area businesses. These sponsoring opportunities can be publicly celebrated between the donor and the student or they can be kept confidential.

Travel permissions follow the strict school district guidelines. Time is a friend when orchestrating major student trips. Depend on competent staff members to keep the organization and obligations related to time. As with the previous section, parents may be an untapped resource in a school. Ask their advice in funding these post-secondary resources. They may be willing to contribute or "sponsor a student" or even chaperone. Others will donate to avoid the long car ride with teenagers to explore multiple universities.

Parents, staff or other educators may claim that if a child is so bright, why do they need to be served with university experiences. Again, why should limited resources be spent on a gifted student who is obviously college bound. First of all, this is an erroneous claim. All gifted students do not go to college. Like all students, they need encouragement and direction from those who respect them and their abilities. The answer from the wise champion of advanced learners is that their needs are as critical and vast as other students. Their needs count and will be met by their school leader.

Another low-cost opportunity is to create a mentoring program between college students and a school's kindergarten through high school students. These College Buddies can be recruited through education programs from the local universities or colleges. These mentors visit their mentees for lunch or planned receptions and activities. A field trip to the colleges includes personalized tours and a college sponsored lunch with their College Buddy.

Our school counselor advised me there has been double the instances of students in her office with intentions to harm themselves, or others, so far this school year.

And, it's only October!

An observant and caring school leader notices when their students are experiencing a difficulty. The first experience in navigating the barriers of possible supervisory responses and "permissions" to implement an innovative program teaches the school administrator their level of tenacity and how to effectively raise the bar in meeting student needs. The support staff knows the leader's caring nature and reports important situations to receive advice and support.

In this scenario, the school counselor alerted the administrator she was noticing a trend of students arriving in her office with intentions to harm themselves. Furthermore, several students reported to her there were other students having similar thoughts and would not come to her office. The immediate response is to peel back the layers of each situation and investigate why the students are struggling.

The school counselor and administrator review the situations for similarities and find the majority are high level learners. The teacher assigned for gifted support is brought into the team to brainstorm on the reason for the trend. It is found the students are experiencing multiple levels of stress and pressure academically and socially. The school leader determines the students need experts to support their delicate needs. Serving the students at this level of need was beyond the scope of the school counselor or the gifted support teacher.

The solution, which involved parent permissions, is to bring qualified counselors to the school to meet with individuals and groups of students. A call to the itinerate psychologist assigned to the school, revealed that her caseload and responsibilities at multiple schools precluded her from spending the required time with these students. However, she gave several options to pursue to meet their needs.

The first suggestion was to ask each parent to take their child to private counseling. Of course, this solution was already in place with the most severe cases. However, the majority of the borderline students did not have this option due to a lack of insurance, citizenship or parental support. These students needed an in-house counselor.

The second suggestion was to pay for an independent, school district approved mental health specialist to visit the school for a specific period of time each week. The students would be pulled out individually or in groups for discussions after parent permissions were granted. This method of serving the students in need of social and emotional support was preferred.

The third suggestion was for her to meet with the students when she had the time. Which was about once a month. This was not acceptable to the school team. These students needed support more often. Of course, students who were in critical need would be referred to a specialist immediately.

The school leader started chasing the funds to pay for the independent psychologist's time. A request for district funding included the data on the frequency of issues and the student demographics, including their identification as gifted and the family economic situation. The district recommended the third suggestion with the request for funds and additional personnel denied.

This is a critical crossroad for the school leader. Accept the supervisor and psychologist's rationale and carry out their suggestion. Or, seek the solution which the school team knew was best for their students. The administrator's supervisor cautiously approved this initiative in pursuing the second option.

Money is a frequent and strong barrier in appropriately serving children. It takes the advice of multiple people who understand and believe in the school leader's plight to find a solution. These experts are a "wealth" of knowledge on how to proceed. Remember, most school leaders arrive to their current position from a classroom or other professional education experiences. There are few school administrators with a business or entrepreneurial mindset.

The collaborative conversation led the leader to take successful action. One of the first steps was to communicate the school's plight with the approved district psychologists. It was irrelevant if the number to contact was two or fifty. Bingo, one of the qualified and approved psychologists was willing to provide services at a greatly reduced rate. Incredibly, she was working with an intern who was qualified and wanted to volunteer.

While the school leader was researching and confirming the psychologists, the school counselor and Gifted Specialist were contacting parents for permissions. They also met with students to learn their opinion and suggestions on the initiative. The students communicated their concerns and appreciation for the opportunity. An alive and active school grapevine added more students to the list of need.

The school leader's last step was to find the funds to pay the reduced rate of the psychologist. A strong determination to not charge the families paid off. As in the previous scenarios, the internal budgets were reviewed with new, critical eyes. Another bingo, the social studies department had an internal account with over ten-thousand dollars. These funds were the result of a retired faculty member's donation upon their departure. The fund had not been accessed in over five years.

A short meeting with the social science department leader brought their willingness to use the funds for the initiative. An ethical leader will not move forward until the original donor agrees to the unique use of their donated funds. The school leader visited with the retired donor and explained the situation. He not only agreed but asked to be an active part in serving the students.

The next step was to gain written permission from all the players: the donor, social science leader, and the district supervisors. The funds were now legally and appropriately utilized to fund the mental health initiative with a watertight paper trail. Barriers were possible at each juncture of this process. If any of the permissions were not granted, the school leader would turn and find another road toward implementation.

The last step has two important elements. The first is for the school leader to inform their staff they have the funding and to start scheduling the meetings with students. This is a student champion moment. The staff sees the resiliency of their leader to serve students.

The second element is to publicize the program. This process brings positive attention to the school for supervisors, parents, students, business partners and naysayers. Knowing the social science funding will run out, this publicity is partnered with fertilizing the soil for harvesting future contributors. Public relations are an important element of the school leader's job description.

Reading Discussion Activities

1. Discuss past experiences that were impacted by barriers to innovative suggestions.
2. Describe the initiatives your school leader has attempted but was stopped by a supervising authority or other reason.
3. Brainstorm student-centered initiatives that would improve your gifted learners' education. Next, write an action plan to ensure their approval and implementation.

CHAPTER 11

The Parent of the Gifted:

Tread Lightly and Navigate for Success

The parent of the high-level learner is considered a part of the student advocate team along with the administration, counselors, teachers, support persons, etc. Each has an important role in propelling the student to the top of their abilities. The characteristics of the parent are recognized as they navigate the school systems for their children.

A parent has the power to confidentially voice their concern to the school leader to orchestrate change. With this information, the leader is given insight into how to better serve all students. Listen to engaged parents through their lens and learn. In turn, explain the lens of an administrator. Work together to build a positive learning environment for all children.

Listen to and give support to parents

The parent of a gifted student may not have a history of involvement in their child's education. The child is thriving, and no intervention has been needed. Yet, when an event occurs, they arrive at the doorstep of the school leader. For example, the student earns their first "B" during a grading period. The school administrator has the responsibility of knowing their teacher's routines and expectations. By encouraging the parent to communicate directly with the teacher, the parent learns the details of the grading process. This frequently occurs in transition years from elementary to middle school and from middle school to high school. It is during these times when expectations change, and more challenging academic work is assigned.

High School Principal: *I was alerted that an angry parent was waiting for me to return their call today. The mother was polite, but stern. She was sticking up for her gifted daughter who received a "B" grade on her science lab. Her explanation was well thought out. In the end, she told me her daughter had never received a B in science prior to this teacher's class. Her 9th grader was destined to attend an ivy league university and pursue nuclear biology. It was obviously the teacher's actions and grading method that were flawed. I had been in this teacher's classroom many times. She is tough, but fair. I listened and reassured the parent that her daughter is on track and will learn a great deal from this effective teacher who will, undoubtedly be one of her favorites by the end of the school year.*

Conversely, the parent of a gifted student may be highly engaged in all aspects of their education. The school leader is wise to keep this parent's telephone number close and call with updates and concerns. For example, a parent requests notification of all homework assignments and tests. They also request that the teacher remind their child to turn in their homework. This will occur when classroom procedures require students to place homework in a basket or folder upon arriving to class. The decision to meet this request is the teacher's choice, not the school leader. A positive school leader encourages parents to vent to them, while protecting such venting to their teachers.

More than just a parent, they are also child advocates

There is a psychological element to serving parents. The school leader enjoys from 20 to 2,000 students or more. Most of their behaviors are predictable to the veteran administrator. Yet, a parent may have little experience with schools and even with raising their one or two children. Their experiences are unique to them as they navigate the needs of their children within a complex school system. For example, the "white knight" complex shows itself when a child is close to graduation. The mother or father ride to their child's rescue to prove they are still viable as a parent. Involve the student in these situations. A wise school leader will give the "white knight" an opportunity to win the battle while staying within the school rules and expectations.

Middle School Principal: *I received a text around dinner time from one of my student's parents. She advised me that she had received several calls from other parents about a situation which occurred in Ms. Helm's classroom that day at school. I told her I was aware of what occurred and had started an investigation. I put some notes together on our plan to deal with the situation. Without this parent's warning, I would have not been prepared to meet the group of parents arriving at my door the next morning at 7am.*

Develop or join a gifted-student parent network

Involve the parents in the school activities and committees. A close relationship with the parents of gifted children will produce positive results for all child advocates on the team. The parent network holds great potential in advocating for a school leader's initiatives. Know which parents to contact to take the "temperature" of a situation. In turn, they will keep a trusted administrator informed of the communication on the parent grapevine.

Students vary in their desire to have active parents in their school environment. Protecting student privacy and learning to discern the child's relationship with their parents is an important element in serving individual students. For example, high level learners may be shy and avoid recognition for their accomplishments. Their parents may disagree and request great fanfare for their child's accomplishments. The wise administrator knows how to serve the student by either publicizing or keeping accolades quiet.

Parent of Gifted 4th Grader: *I know the rules. There are no late forms accepted for field trips. I knew I was taking a chance going to the school to see the principal to plea for mercy. She met me in her office and listened to me explain how my* *child is the World Class Procrastinator and did not turn in the form for the prized field trip. It was in his backpack. He is so unorganized and forgetful. The principal was so kind. She knew my child and she still accepted the form. Of course, I promised to not breathe a word to the other parents. I can't tell you how much this meant to me as a parent. I am so glad my two children have such a caring principal.*

Celebrating a child's needs and uniqueness while serving the needs of their parents is a tightrope. There is no set rule or guideline when working with parents. Each situation demands the school leader balance the needs of the student with the needs of their parents. Altering a past decision at a parent's request may provide a more productive future than holding strong to that decision. Know when to "hold 'em and when to fold 'em," (Don Schlitz, recorded by Kenny Rogers) but always be available and present for parents.

Part Three includes for further resources for the parents of gifted students and school leaders.

Reading Discussion Activities

1. Describe in detail, an issue you experienced with a parent of a gifted child. Using the content of this chapter, how could you have applied these tools to improve the situation?
2. From your viewpoint as a school leader, list the top 10 priorities of a gifted parent.
3. What advice would you give to a new school administrator who has yet to encounter a parent of a gifted student who is unhappy with how their child is served in your school.

Chapter 12
Creating a School Infrastructure to Grow Opportunities Outside of the School Day

The school environment has the potential to be mastered by a gifted student. The teachers, classes, subjects, etc. have a natural predictability in the nation's school systems. Stretching the acceleration components of the academic offerings helps to address these needs for more academic stimulation for gifted students. However, there are additional platforms for a student to experience applied higher-level learning environments.

Mine the internal school environment for high level experiences. For example, middle school students can mentor elementary students in a prescribed and well-organized program. These transitional mentor programs build confidence in each student, relieve the anxiety of moving to middle school, stretch the nurturing capacity of the middle schooler, and build cross grade-level friendships which can last through graduation.

Furthermore, the middle school student will thrive under the careful watch of their high school mentor. Students identified as gifted share unique abilities and personalities. This partnership propels a more confident middle school student into the high school environment with a readiness to succeed. Creating these purposeful partnerships is accomplished through student interest surveys conducted at both schools. Pairing students who share interests in band, chess, robotics, languages, etc. starts the relationship on a common footing.

Partnerships with Community and Business

The adult world encompasses businesses that provide an external opportunity for personal and academic growth. Secondary students are provided with opportunities to explore careers through mentorships, job shadowing, field trips, etc. These experiences are organized through business partnerships. The relationships are initiated and built by the school administration and teachers.

Many schools conduct Community Partner Fairs to introduce students to various businesses that are interested in partnering with schools. Students may also select their preferred business through elective choices or their own exploration. The school follows safety policies by managing all aspects of the mentorships, job shadowing and any interaction with the outside entity. Students are exposed to non-academic environments and learn to apply their academic skills while learning the many facets of a professional organization.

The school leader has the ability to champion active business partnerships for all levels of learners. It is important to include gifted students in this process by realizing their priorities. They may choose an internship over a high academic course if the content and weight is attractive.

Seek out secondary course descriptions for internships which have weighted credits. This is similar to honors or Advanced Placement weighting. These higher-level courses with weighted credits will appeal to gifted students who are shopping for a high-grade point average.

Many of these courses are not required to be taken in succession. Skipping the entry level classes and taking a weighted upper level course will please the advanced student. They will thrive in the business environment by learning diverse skills. Their eyes will be opened to how the organizational structure of a business is drastically different from a classroom or an easy elective.

Gifted Senior Student: *I wasn't sure about taking a business class instead of AP Psychology, but I thought it would be different, so I gave it a try. Part of the class requirement is to intern at a business. I went to a marketing firm. I expected it to be fun, all professional and everything. But I did not* *expect to be treated like an adult. I did not have to ask to go to the bathroom. I had an idea and when they asked me how I would solve the problem, I gave my idea. They listened to me! I would say I learned "applied psychology." Plus, I learned so much more about what I want to take in college.*

Campus activities that impact a lifetime

School leaders will align student interests (review student elective registration) with campus organizations which provide students with high level and relevant experiences. For example, members of the Health Occupations Student Association (HOSA) learn leadership and medical skills through regional, state and national competitions. Advanced students may not enroll into the school's medical oriented courses due to their tight academic schedules. Yet, they actively participate in HOSA with various academic levels of students with similar interests.

The Career and Technical Education Student Organizations[1]

Organization	Focus	Members	Chapters
Business Professionals of America (BPA)	Leadership, citizenship, gaining academic & technical skills in Business & Management Administration, Finance, Information & Technology	45,000	1,800
DECA	Themes of Entrepreneurship and 21st Century Employability Skills applied through: Business Management & Administration, Finance, Hospitality & Tourism and Marketing	215,000	3,500
Educators Rising	Preparing members for careers in the teaching profession	43,000	2,400
Family, Career and Community Leaders of America (FCCLA)	Career exploration and leadership development in Culinary Arts, Education & Training, Hospitality & Tourism and Human Services	160,000	5,300

Organization	**Focus**	**Members**	**Chapters**
Future Business Leaders of America (FBLA)	Prepare students to become community-minded business leaders with emphasis on Business Management & Administration, Finance, Information Technology and Marketing	230,000	5,200
Health Occupation Student Association (HOSA)	"Promote career opportunities in the health care industry and to enhance the delivery of quality health care to all people"	200,000	3,500
National FFA Organization (FFA)	Dedicated to preparing students for careers in Agriculture, Food and Natural Resources with a focus on leadership and communication	669,000	8,630
Skills USA	Workplace and personal skills with technical skills grounded in academics, applicable to any career pathway	360,000	19,000
Technology Student Association (TSA)	Science, technology, engineering and mathematics: the mission is to "enhance personal development, leadership and career opportunities"	250,000	2,000

CTSA: Career Technical Student Organization, https://www.aeseducation.com/blog/career-technical-student-organization-ctso

It is the school leader who supports and encourages teachers to sponsor and fully participate in such organizations. These experiences and accolades are not only assets on a college application, but the advanced student completes their secondary education with a greater understanding of their chosen college major and ultimate career. Additionally, the club activities showcase the school in the business community.

Reading Discussion Activities

1. As an adult, describe how your own school and professional life experiences may have been differed if you were provided with the career courses and clubs in secondary school.
2. Write out the conversation you would have with parent who is questioning why a career-oriented class or club is better for their student than an additional high-level academic course or academic-related club.
3. List the potential business partners, clubs, teachers and other details that apply to your school in determining how to embed these valuable courses and clubs into your school.

Chapter 13
Informed and Supportive Gifted and Student-Centered School Counselors

A popular myth about children identified as gifted is they do not need counselor support. Regardless of grade level, counselors are often the gatekeepers of a student's future. They hold the key to the academic and elective schedules, provide a "soft place to land" in a school and have the power to support an advanced learner when other student advocates fail.

Knowledgeable school leaders are aware counselor responsibilities have increased 10-fold in the last decade. Scheduling, testing, counseling, conferencing has all increased. In addition, they are responsible for knowing and understanding every disability and exceptionality of their assigned students.

School Counselors are people too

The School Counselor's time is their greatest and most limited resource. Consequently, they are frequently asked to make students who are at risk of not graduating their top priority. The gifted student is often left to survive without one-on-one time with their school counselor. But their needs are vast.

Secondary School Counselor: *I received a call from one of my senior's parents. She said she wanted her daughter to be put back into an AP Government class for the second semester of her senior year. The student was adamant she wanted out of the* *class just a few weeks ago. She had already been accepted at a state university, so she had to send her updated second semester schedule after she dropped AP Government. Apparently, the university wrote her a letter rescinding her acceptance. I was so surprised! I asked her parent to email me the letter. With her permission, I passed to other counselors in the district and my supervisors. I am so glad I have a good relationship with both the student and the parent. This information will help so many other students in the future. Building trust!*

A school's culture is sensed in the school counselor offices. A positive counseling environment values intellectual discovery and unique opportunities to thrive in and out of the classroom. A counselor has the power to research and present a plethora of opportunities to students at every grade level. They cast light on the various acceleration models, business internships and early university enrollment, to name just a few items in their knowledge base. An open and exploratory counselor's office radiates a positive energy.

The impact of a School Counselor is schoolwide

A gifted student-centered school counselor is proactive in setting up successful situations for students. School administrators encourage training in a wide range of exceptional abilities among their brightest students. This knowledge increases their flexibility in addressing individual exceptionalities through supportive systems.

School leaders with knowledge of the power a counselor has in building student capacity will utilize their time wisely. Requiring at least one counselor to be present at student lunches is an effective use of their time. Students of all academic levels have access to a counselor without missing class. Additionally, this turns into a relationship building affair as students crowd in to get their "counselor time." It is not unusual for a counselor to have a greater understanding of a student's learning needs than their parents, or even their teachers.

8th Grader: *My counselor is in the cafeteria during our lunch on Tuesdays and Thursdays. Lots of students crowd around and talk to her about silly stuff. I'm not one of them. But she really helped me out on my high school electives. I had no idea what to take. I had to go to her like five times to get it right. My mom kept sending me questions to ask her. She asked me why I changed lunch tables. I didn't think she would notice stuff like that. We talked about it later. Yes, I am glad she is always there with us on Tuesdays and Thursdays. It made it easier.*

A well-trained counselor in gifted education will advise students and their families on talent development opportunities. Their advice will include information about academic talent searches, academic competitions, summer academic programs and scholarships. Elementary parents may need additional resources on how to keep their newly identified gifted child academically toned.

Student surveys reveal the truth

It is recommended that a student survey is conducted each school year. This survey provides the teacher, administrator, counselor and other student advocates with a list of the student's interests, goals and concerns. Conduct the survey late in the school year when students have experiences to share and are confident about their answers. To be clear, this is a student interest survey. Other types of surveys to consider are course evaluations, mental health and bullying, school climate, or faculty evaluation surveys. Counselors can conduct the surveys, disaggregate the information and pass it on to the teachers with their exceptionality accommodations.

Below is an example of questions for an annual *Student Interest Survey* with open comment questions. A quality survey will be announced as confidential, include 25+ questions, and conducted during the school day (not prior to lunch or dismissal). Each question can be adapted to a Likert scale with the addition of 4+ answer choices for each item.

2020 Lead Smart High School Student Interest Survey	
Years attending LSHS:	**Grade Level:**
1	What is your favorite class and why?
2	What classes would you like to take?? You may list classes not currently offered at school.
3	Given a chance, what is the one change you would make at your school?
4	What makes you proud of your school?
5	How much time do you spend on homework each day?
6	What are your proudest school-based achievements and why?
7	What are 3 things your teachers can do to encourage your learning and participating in school?
8	What is the most important activity your counselor can do for you?
9	List 3 things that make you want to come to school.
10	List 3 careers of interest to you in order of your preference.

School leaders can encourage the use of the student information in classroom procedures, assignments, course offerings and accommodations. Of course, these interest surveys are used by school leaders to determine the addition of school courses, clubs, etc.

A school leader is advised to be present in the counselor office and lead brief weekly informative meetings with all the counselors. These meetings are family circles to discuss (and vent about) students, parents, teachers and procedures. It is the school leader's responsibility to listen for trends and pending issues and proactively address each for the counselors. The agenda always includes naming students in danger of not graduating.

A gifted-centered school administrator stays apprised of their counselors' focus. They inquire how counselors are meeting the needs of students at the top of the school's academic scale. The counselor assists students in recognizing who they are, make decisions and develop to their full potential.[1] This counselor-school administrator relationship has a similar impact as building the school's master schedule.

High School Principal: *Molly came into my office late one afternoon. She was one of our top senior students, a bit shy, but always sweet and confident. She needed my permission to drop her AP Biology class. She earned a B for the first quarter of the two-quarter semester. Our school rule was that the principal had to give permission to drop any AP class. Students drop classes for non-academic reasons, and this gave me a chance to encourage them to stay. Molly said she had never received a B during any grading period, ever, since kindergarten. I knew the teacher was highly rigorous, yet predictable. I asked Molly what she would study at the university. She said she was going to be a surgeon. Really? No, she was not granted permission to drop the class. That was almost 10 years ago. Molly just graduated medical school and is now in a cardiology residency.*

The gifted-student centered counselor is well organized and predictable. Advanced students thrive on predictability that relieves their stress. As soon as possible, post in hardcopy outside an office and on the school's website: calendars of important deadlines and events, registration procedures and expectations, course descriptions, testing schedules, holidays, staff days, and other pertinent dates.

School Counselor: *Cindy was one of my favorites. She was always into school activities. Well, if you call peaceful protests and fund raising for human rights causes a school activity. As with all my top students, she filled out her college applications early. Her selected college was a local small private parochial university. This was a top school but was not a fit for Cindy. She listened to me as I explained how her choice may cause her undue stress during her academic pursuits. I gave her several other in-state options to consider. She visited with her parents and arrived at my door with a new plan. This one fit Cindy. I feel like we dodged a bullet on that one.*

A talented counselor of gifted children has an instinct on how to serve their unique needs. A vast knowledge discerns both the academic and the social and emotional needs of each student. How to accelerate is a frequent conversation in a counselor's office between students and parents.

The knowledgeable counselor will provide the acceleration models with their positive and negative aspects. Some options include skipping a grade level, taking advanced classes, taking early college or online accelerated courses. The parent and the student may differ on how to accelerate. The counselor needs to be savvy of what the student wants and the motivations of the parent to provide the best counsel.

Reading Discussion Activities

1. Create a school counselor vision statement.
2. Generate a survey for your school's counselors. The survey will determine what they know about serving high level learners. Include questions on what they need related to training, time, student access, parent support, etc.
3. Describe how your school will train school counselors to better serve gifted students.

Chapter 14
Remain Aware of the Unique Social and Emotional Needs of the Advanced Learner

School administrators who listen to a student-centered counselor will learn how to serve the needs of their brightest students. A common intrapersonal trait is the ability to keep their feelings to themselves. A gifted student decides when and if they allow others to know their thoughts. Often, their trials include the unwritten rules of a gifted classroom or their advanced peer group. These high expectations on grades, behavior, and projects can be overwhelming. A savvy counselor or teacher will notice these stressors and find tools to address the issues.

The advanced student's peer group has a strong structure built around academic competition. The classroom can become a "Lord of the Flies" scenario if left unchecked by teachers and counselors. Built-in collaborative structures build trust and a feeling of teamwork within these competitive classrooms.

The ability to effectively work in groups is essential for life, college preparation and professional careers. These collaborative structures build confidence in a unique student as they contribute their talents to their team. A master schedule can be built to encourage collaborative structures. A school leader, their counselors and the teachers have the ability to model this collaborative learning environment through training, their presence, advice, etc.

A school leader and support staff with an understanding of the intrapersonal facets of the gifted mindset can build a positive school environment. Without this understanding, the advanced learner will not excel to the top of their abilities. For example, there is a glass ceiling on ability in some cultures. The group performance is held in high regard, where the "tribe" is more important than the individual. To a gifted student this translates into resisting stretching toward top performances. They will purposefully sabotage their experiences to stay with the group.

A Classroom of Gifted Individuals can be Highly Competitive

The Frog Pond Theory enhances this competitiveness as it encourages students to outperform their classmates. Yet, when one of the students fails to keep up with the accelerating packs, the reaction of the other students is often exclusion from participation in groups. Students are aware of each other's academic abilities, grades, etc. It takes purposeful teacher intervention to avoid this shunning in highly competitive gifted classrooms.

A successful parent or student conference is unique for advanced learners. The school leader or assistant school leader joins the counselor and teachers. Specialists are invited as they relate to the student's exceptionalities. This practice of including school administration meets several objectives. First, the leader's knowledge of the school's procedures, master schedule, past situations with the same student, etc. provide a support system for the teachers, student, parent and counselor present. Second, the school leaders learn the teacher's classroom procedures, expectations, etc. This is valuable information for future interactions with students and parents. Third, the counselor and teachers feel their support when a parent is less than polite with their opinions. A school leader's role is to protect the professionalism in a conference.

> ***School Leader during a gifted student conference:*** *All my students are brilliant. But Lucy is over the top smart. The conference was filled with her teachers, both parents and our school counselor. As we went around the table to determine why she was not succeeding in class, Lucy articulated in great*

detail why she earned her present grade in each class. I learned quickly when working with advanced learners that they know exactly why they don't have the "A." They know how to get the top grade. That is not the issue. Getting them motivated is why we are here—to support them through these tough times.

A student-conference is recommended over a parent-conference. Even the youngest of children has the ability to engage in an insightful dialogue concerning their academic and behavioral progress. Students are the center of the discussion in a student conference. This seems redundant to a parent conference. However, the administrator leads the conference (models for the counselor for future conferences) with an inquiry about the student's opinions on the reasons for their progress or lack of progress. The student provides information. The gifted student will provide a pragmatic answer. The parent is an observer and involved when the team determines corrective actions need support in the home.

Society's Perspective of the High Achieving Student

In the beginning pages of this book the term "gifted" was defined by multiple sources. The high ability and talented students are identified as having unique educational needs. Their demonstration of higher aptitude levels requires resources targeted at their learning needs. An informed school leader seeks opportunities to meet these unique needs. An informed school leader who does not look for these shifts is choosing to harmfully ignore the needs of these students.

The small shifts made to better serve the gifted student population are outlined in these pages. The broad federal guideline for Gifted Education only provides a general suggestion on how to serve gifted students. The decision of a school leader to avoid shifts or adaptations harms the brightest students in the school. A student not learning at their full capacity is a victim of education negligence when small cost effect measures exist.

Positive societal and institutional changes in gifted education are occurring slowly across the nation. It takes knowledgeable and motivated school administrators to change a gifted student's future. Their ability to recognize, build and implement innovative gifted education services is a model to the parents and the student.

The barriers will appear in serving the gifted student due to bias and prejudices. These children are seen as self-sufficient. They will graduate without additional resources. This is the lowest common denominator, not the highest. Yet, these societal prejudices will build barriers for the innovative leader.

Serving the Underserved Students Identified as Gifted

What is the traditional method of identifying gifted and talented students? Parent and teacher referrals in the early grades are the most common across the United States. These gatekeeper-type of recommendations limit diversification.

These traditional methodologies tend to favor middle class English speakers and rely on local norms, rather than national norms. Talent is overlooked with the referral systems. Remember, our high achieving students are one of the nation's most valuable resources. Find them in the school and give them support.

Education advocates use student data to press for change in the identification trends of our gifted students. Researchers, practitioners and citizens concerned with societal inequity continually seek an improved and equitable identifier. Universal screening at different age levels is one option for combating the disproportionality of the current screening practices.[1]

High School Assistant Principal over Student Discipline: *Bradly was to meet with me and his parent because of his outbursts during our high stakes state testing. I knew Bradly from past discipline issues. They all involved his choice to not follow school rules. I watched as his mom was dropped off from an older car that left immediately. Mom was obviously experiencing financial difficulties. We sat at my little conference table and I asked Bradley to explain what happened. He used the "F" word in his description. I stopped him and reminded him we don't use that word here in the conference. He* *apologized. It slipped out again and my look elicited another apology. This was his vernacular. It was the day report cards were distributed and I asked for it. Straight A's. This was my surprise. After the conference I researched and found he has a 130 IQ. Bradley had never been screened for gifted. This was taken care of immediately and Bradley was provided support for his amazing brain. This is a child I will never forget. His behavior still bubbled up occasionally, but he was placed on a track that could change his family legacy.*

So, how is a more diverse pool of students identified as gifted in a school? Screen *eligible* students and not just referred students. Eligible students have revealing data from achievement tests, classroom observations, class grades, and even other cognitive-related assessments. Screen in later school years. Transitional students may have missed their opportunities to screen in previous schools.

Take a close look at the screening instrument. These instruments utilized for identification may also hold a bias against the non-English speaking children. Underrepresented students need to experience enrichment instruction prior to the screening to understand the instrument fully.

The school leader holds the power to make universal screening happen for the children in their school. Make the search for gifted and talented students a goal of the administration team. All school staff are referred to as "talent scouts" and are familiar with identifying students. Yes, there are costs and multiple barriers. As with other student-centered initiatives, turn over the rocks and find the funding.

Reading Discussion Activities

1. Describe a gifted student you know and how the Frog Pond Theory relates to their learning experiences in your school.
2. Brainstorm the specific actions a school leader or advocate can take to address the competitive spirit of an advanced learner in school and out of school.
3. Write out a step-by-step plan on how your school is going to address the underserved students in gifted education. Include a timeline and delegated tasks.

Closing Comments of Encouragement

The role of a school leader is to meet the needs of all students from all backgrounds and abilities in their school. By becoming aware of the ultimate nurturing academic environment for the gifted student, the school leader has the knowledge to not only meet their needs but propel these amazing young people into a more successful future. Knowledge is power. Tenacity to change the status quo and listen to the experts takes energy to plan and resiliency when barriers occur.

The inset scenarios *in this section* reveal the real people behind a school leader's decisions. Lives are altered, transformed and improved by a few well-orchestrated shifts from the top. Be innovative in providing students with personalized resources that give them the tools for success as they discover their true potential.

The national, state and district entities which ground a school's policies and procedures, from laws to the calendar, are there for all school leaders to follow. It is a manager who simply follows these foundational expectations to keep their school afloat. It is a leader who stands firmly on this foundation while designing innovative student-centered initiatives that directly impact the lives of all levels of their young learners.

Part Three

Parenting Gifted Children from the Perspective of a School Leader: It Takes Patience, Knowledge and a Village

Coming together is a beginning;
keeping together is progress;
working together is success.

Henry Ford (American Industrialist,
founder of Ford Motor Company, 1963 – 1947)

Introduction to Part Three

These chapters provide the parents of high achievers with a look into the school leader's world. They also provide the school leader with a clearer vision of what the parents of their students need from schools. Each section brings the parent and the school leader to a closer understanding of each other. The importance of this relationship cannot be understated.

Part One and *Part Two* focused on building a gifted student-centered school infrastructure. *Part Three* focuses on the academic, social and emotional needs of the gifted child from the lens of a gifted child advocate. Read each chapter in a quest to learn how to help a child as well as a school leader break down barriers.

The theme of *Part Three* is the encouragement of parents of gifted children. Seek out knowledge, solutions, camaraderie and truth in the child's education. The servant leader will show their appreciation for the opportunity to serve high achieving students and their families through their actions. Encourage this partnership.

The scenarios are taken from leadership experiences that are true to life and occur in almost every school. Each reader has their own stories to tell. Use these examples as additional information to formulate solutions for all children in their home and at school.

Many parents have the opportunity to select their child's school. Select a school with visionary leaders. Visit and walk through the halls with the administration while seeking an explanation of the curriculum and school operations. Listen to their wisdom. State your concerns and past experiences. Action and measurable results are the goal. Be a partner. Understand the lay of the land and the school's organizational structure. Be aware of barriers. Listen for key words. Talk with other parents, listen only to the problem solvers not the naysayers.

Parents build their relationship with their children from birth, through the school years and beyond. Yet school leaders enjoy the child for a snapshot in their life. This is the time to work together to make a lifelong difference. This partnership of quality collaboration and communication creates a higher functioning graduate. The desired result is a gifted adult who has the tools and experiences to effectively meet life's future challenges.

Explore these *Part Three* chapters and know it is possible for all school leaders to actively and purposely serve advanced learners within any school structure.

Chapter 15
Can You Accurately Describe an Advanced Learner?

It depends on who is describing...

Parents with more than one child or have the opportunity to be close to multiple children will notice differences in their characteristics, learning styles and overall personalities. These differences change and stay the same with age. Enter a school of other students and the differences are exaggerated and noticeable by all. The question is "what causes these differences?" And, should there be interventions or is this just a childhood event.

Astute school leaders of all grade levels will notice the difference in their student populations. Each of their students are budding humans who hold unique abilities, needs, and perspectives. The same student will grow into a different person from day to day or year to year. A generalization of the character and needs of a particular "type" of student is a trap. A quality school administrator treats generalizations like kryptonite. And shudders when others apply these generalized statements to the children in their school. Why? Because a child may have the general identifying characteristics of a certain type of student (gifted), but the deeper individualistic persona impacts this generalization. When working with parents of any student, they do not want to hear a school leader's generalization about their child. They are passionately aware of the uniqueness of their child. Their child is different from any student who has entered the school because this is their child.

Parents of gifted students can experience a rollercoaster of events both enjoyable and challenging. Educators have a responsibility to know how to support these high achievers. Engaging with their parents helps those who do not fully understanding what appears to be laziness may have other causes for a lack of motivation. An administrator's knowledge of the characteristics and needs of the high achiever are pragmatically applied to the current parental exchange of the moment. The young student's individuality is paramount to any prior knowledge or relevant research. This section capitalizes on this student-centered framework as applied to parenting gifted children.

A Parent Describes their Gifted Child

Ask a parent to describe their gifted child and the answers will both differ from and match other parents. They may start with the strengths. Their child has amazing and unique qualities. These strengths are where an administrator begins when advising parents. Remember each individual student's strength. The weaknesses will be described as both actions and assumptions. Their child may be described as highly unorganized and messy, yet the 7th grader can write computer code after taking one free online Harvard University course. Their child may be described as woefully hard on themselves with overt perfectionist tendencies, yet easily bring other children together on a communitywide successful philanthropy project.

Beginning with a student's strengths, a student conference provides an applicable school-based demonstration for parents. The conference may be arranged to discuss a decline in grades, a behavior issue or any student driven issue. The place to start with is the student's strength. Every gifted student has strengths. If the leader of the conference does not know the student's strengths, ask the student and parent for their opinions at the beginning of the conference. This method of conferencing encourages the student by displaying a positive, nurturing atmosphere. The negative issues causing the conference are next but use the child's strengths to find solutions. Additionally, a potentially concerned parent will appreciate the school's knowledge and caring about their child.

Parent Scenario: *John is my second. He crawled earlier than his big sister. But that was not when we knew he was different. He "worked" with me in the yard and in my garage since he could walk. He seemed to enjoy fiddling with my tools. I came home from work one day and the garage air compressor was in about 30 pieces on the floor of my garage. He had removed the cylinder head, and was covered in oil and dirt, my tools were all over the floor. He was 5 years old at the time. I called him out to the garage and told him to put it back together. We were at dinner the next night and I asked him why he took it apart. He said he wanted to see how the air came out and how it worked. I reminded him to put it back together. He said matter-of-factly that he already fixed it. What? I don't know how an air compressor works, but my 5-year-old can build one.*

Ask a parent to describe what their gifted child's needs to succeed and the answers may differ from the educator's opinion. This is delicate territory. A parent who believes the method of correction (or even encouragement) used on them as a child will work on their child may need more contemporary tools. This generation of students has a vastly different lens of the world than the past generations. The current cohort of students in a grade level is different from the year's prior cohort. Every parent wants their child to succeed in school. The strength of the school leader's knowledge on nurturing the current generation of gifted children is applied gently to the individual child and their parents.

A Gifted Student Describes Themselves

Ask a student identified as gifted how they are different from other students, and the answers vary with each child. Interestingly, their answers almost always start with their strengths. Depending on their grade level and ability to communicate, the gifted child may report they are simply good at studying and applying their knowledge. They report they take less time to understand a concept of a lesson. They may say they are good at math or science. Answers are frequently given as a comparison with a non-gifted sibling or friend.

Student Scenario: *I don't really want to be different. But it just happens. They told me I was gifted in elementary school. Luckily, I have stayed in the same school and the other gifted kids in my class are my friends. There is this one guy, Marcus, who is so weird. But he is smart and funny. The kids in other classes make fun of him. They call him a nerd. He doesn't seem to mind. I know I would. He is our friend. Marcus talks more in our special gifted class and the teacher really likes him. She laughs at his jokes.*

Prod the gifted student to reveal their weaknesses and voices from their environment appear. Their parent may have told them they are a procrastinator or are not applying themselves in all classes. They may repeat a past teacher's comments about their poor penmanship or social skills. The opinions of other children may appear in the form of derogatory terms or name-calling. The school administrator, counselor and parent have the power to listen and encourage their gifted students in adapting to a highly critical world.

A School Leader's Description of the gifted child

Ask a school administrator to define a "gifted student" and the answers are similar across all grade levels. A leader with little specific knowledge of gifted education begins the description with "oh, those are my smart kids." This is truthful, yet narrow. The advanced learners are known for their position at the top of the class in academics. The teachers request them in their classes or desire to be exclusive gifted teachers. There is little parent contact for negative reasons and many of their parents are active in the school environment. These bright students provide the school with great public relations as they win most of the academic contests.

A parent's knowledge of how a school administrator views their gifted child is important in their dealings with the school. This school culture can be perceived through the school's environment. Are there as many academic trophies as athletic trophies displayed? Do after-school, enrichment and extracurricular groups encourage academics? Is there evidence of civics as well as athletics?

The school leader who describes their top learners as incredibly interesting young individuals with special needs indicates they have a working knowledge of the whole child. The communication of their understanding on how to build a school's infrastructure as an asset to the advanced learner reveals the leader's understanding of the gifted child's unique needs and qualities.

Reading Discussion Activities

1. Write out your own definition of a gifted child.
2. Relate an experience with a gifted child that showcases their uniqueness.
3. Who would you go to if you needed an expert opinion on a gifted child. Why?

CHAPTER 16
The "Smart Kid's" Behavior Reflects their Amazing Minds

All parents experience the rollercoasters of joy and occasional wrath as they raise their children. Each age brings a new lesson to be learned in growing a successful well-adjusted adult. Add in the responsibility of raising unusually smart children and a parent is wise to take a deep breath and learn all they can about nurturing their unique children. Disregard parents who claim that it must be so easy to raise a gifted child.

School leaders celebrate the positive characteristics of their gifted children. After years of interactions, the veteran administrator has an awareness of their unique characteristics. The following behaviors are a showcase revealing a small collection of the commonly displayed behaviors in students identified as gifted. This is a short list designed from a school leader's viewpoint to give parents and other advocates an understanding of what an observant educator realizes through interactions with their students.

Points to Ponder About the Advanced Learner

Number one survival skill: find your people (aka. intellectual peer group)

Students are most comfortable with other students similar to themselves. Interaction between students with perceived similarities create strong personal friendships and support.[1] This is a fact at each grade level. The heterogeneous classroom is set up purposefully to integrate all types of learners. This method has its strengths in the socialization of our young people. A school system is frequently built on these principles.

Watch the students. They will seek out students like themselves in their classrooms. The gifted child will notice and socialize with other gifted children. This is human nature. There is no discrimination as to the race, religion, or even age of the other gifted child. These students cluster together and speak the same "advanced learner language."

When making decisions on school choice, consider the gifted learner's "people." Inquire as to how the students are clustered by ability. Make sure the giftedness of the student is nurtured and not diluted into the normalizing of the grade level or team. Also, be wary of inclusion efforts pushed in schools. These children will congregate to their own "people." Be supportive of this organic grouping. Do not deter this activity, encourage it. When a child finds their "people" the parent will see an excitement and an open dialogue about their new friends. This is an exciting time for the child. These similarities will boost self-confidence and achievement.

The parent will notice these groups form with new members entering and less similar students exiting the group. They will want to spend time together outside of school. Their parents become close as they monitor their children, of any age, from afar. Parents of like students communicate the school issues and opportunities. These are powerful parental groups. These students will experience inter-group competitions which propel their grades. The lesser learner is frequently supported to uphold the groups acceleration identity.

The school leader will notice these groups as they break themselves into clusters or mini "tribes" within the social opportunities at school. For example, if random seating is acceptable in a school cafeteria, students self-segregate by these groups at each table. To clarify, these students are mixed by race, grade, disability, gender, and other culturally identifying characteristics. It is inspiring to observe students accept their "people" based on intelligence, and not any physical or other attribute.

School Leader Speaks to 8th Graders Considering her High Achieving High School: *The most important choice you can make is to be with your people. These are other students who are motivated like you and will keep you afloat when you lose your way or get "tired" of trying. High school is no different from finding your people in middle school. You can still be with people like you. But wait, how will you feel when you are not the smartest person in the class? There will be many smart kids in your class. This will make you better. These are your people. They will understand you and your motivations.*

The gifted student who is performing at grade level. Is this underachievement?

Parents of children identified as gifted frequently have an expectation for their child to always perform academically above their peers. This expectation is met with some, or all, subjects during various or all school years. Yet, performances may not meet these expectations. The underachieving child has a story to tell. It is up to the school and the child's parent to discover the story.

First, discover if the child believes they can do the work. Listen to their answer. If it is a "no," then ask why. If the answer is a "yes," then further investigation needs to occur. The National Association for Gifted Children publishes multiple resources on the underachievement of the gifted learner. The reasons are complex, and the solutions do not come easy. Parents are encouraged to keep an open communication with their student, the school and their teachers.[2]

Sample Questions to Discover Why a Student is Underachieving[3]

1. Does the student believe they can do the work?
2. Does the student express that they have control over how well they do on their work?
3. Does the student see value in their work at school?
4. What strategies have been utilized by teachers?

5. Has any school intervention proved to be more successful than others?
6. Are negative stereotypes or social pressures encouraging the child to "not be smart"?
7. Are there particular areas or activities that the child especially likes at school?
8. What does the student talk about when excited?
9. What are the dislikes of the child and what do they find the most difficult?
10. Are boredom behaviors observed at home and, if so, when?

(Adapted from NAGC.org)

These questions are critical for use by a school leader who seeks to understand the mind and characteristics of the high achieving student. They prod deeper into the psyche of the child to determine why they are not excelling. These are tools for parents and administrators to explore a child's reasoning.

The school staff is an active participant in finding solutions for the underachieving gifted student. In general, teachers are the first advocates to communicate there is an issue with their student. The trusted school counselors and gifted specialists have training and abilities to delve into the issue with the student. The parent does not need to be present when their student is speaking with these student advocates. This is an important confidential exchange for all grade levels. The objective is to meet the gifted student's needs by defining the supports needed to excel at the top of their abilities. Clear communication between all persons attempting to solve the issues with the student is essential during this process.

The school leaders are active participants in the exploration of the reasons for underachievement. This starts with hiring and training a staff in gifted advocacy. Each teacher, support person and counselor have an eye of discernment for gifted achievement. The school leader holds the teachers and other staff accountable for meeting the students' needs to achieve and the parents' needs for support.

Those who participate in extra-curricular activities are less likely to under-achieve.

"All work and no play" are not good for kids. All students need interactions with peers outside the classroom environment. This participation in healthy outside activities generates positive social interactions with similar students. Students are encouraged to find a group to join, whether academic, civic or athletic. The student will undoubtedly find a group which is comprised of their "people."

A school leader has the ability to create the extracurricular groups students want in their school. There are several methods to determine student interest. Researching the popular programs in the feeder schools gives insight into what students want in their next school. For example, an active chess club in elementary school will transfer to an active chess club in middle school. Also, student registration sheets for the next school year's courses provide a measurement of their interests through elective selections. For example, students who select robotics and are not placed in the class will likely participate in a robotics extracurricular club.

This social interaction breeds healthy competition and enhances a student's motivations to succeed in school. Additionally, mingling with students who have similar interests, yet are not identified as gifted opens the child's exposure to other students. For example, a student who enters a school's archery program may be exposed to excellent archers who are not in their accelerated classes. Other mixed programs are often found in chess, robotics, gaming, tennis, and civic clubs.

Gifted students are capable of earning good grades without learning foundational skills.

The parent of a gifted student has heard the words of exasperation after attending a class. "I already know this stuff. I am not going to learn anything. Why do I have to do all this busy work?" From a school leader perspective, the child is correct in their assessment of the course. An evaluation on the course is the first step. Is the student properly placed in this academic course? Is acceleration needed to a more difficult course? Or, does the teacher have the tools necessary to augment the curriculum to meet the needs of the gifted student? The answers to these questions will lead to a more appropriate learning environment.

A teacher who teaches *students* and not just the *prescribed curriculum* will recognize the need to enhance a student's learning with their instructional and curricular tools. The individualizing of the daily work and assessments is acceptable. For example, homework may not be a requirement for the student who earns a high grade on each formative assessment. The teacher determines how to make these percentages work in their gradebook. The only caveat is to ensure the student has an understanding of the required material as evidenced through the summative assessments.

The encouragement of the school leader to vary from the standard prescribed curriculum and assignments is essential. Teachers have the professional license to adapt lessons. They can forgive assignments based on the student's prior knowledge. Also, outlaw worksheets for high level learners. There are students who learn through worksheets, but these are rarely advanced learners.

Depending on the age of the student, they may need to self-advocate in their quest to experience an adapted curriculum in their class. It takes confidence to respectfully ask the teacher to be excused from the daily work or what they may term "busy work." Understand that this practice is uncommon and depends on the teacher's grace in approving such deviations from the norm in their class. A respectful student also meets each deadline and performs their best on all course work regardless of the teacher's final decision to adapt the assignments.

These classroom situations provide the parent of the high achiever with opportunities to learn how to adapt to group situations. They know they are different as they watch their classmates struggle with the class expectations. This learned knowledge of their unique intelligence is used to differentiate them from others in a positive and accepting manner. Parents may use this opportunity to celebrate their intelligence while encouraging them to accept the diversities in their peers.

Teacher of Advanced Placement US History: *Sarah completed each assignment and participated in our 90-minute class periods in the first quarter. I assigned the chapter to be read at home, prior to teaching the content in class. Following a short reading quiz when they entered class, we had a brief lecture. Following the quiz and lecture, students worked in groups to delve deeper into the concepts prior to an assessment the next class. This was our routine and Sarah learned quickly that if she read the chapter, she did not need to listen to the lecture. She enjoyed participating in the group work and earned "A's" on all our assessments. So, I had to decide whether to force her to put her reading book down during my lecture. She was so sweet when I spoke with her about it. She said she enjoyed the content but preferred to learn it at home. She is my example of adapting my expectations to the individual. I enjoyed having her in class. Sarah learned the material and did not have the same needs as the other students.*

My gifted child never seems to encounter a situation where self-discipline and study skills are needed.

A parent will listen to their child's assessment of the school day when they return home from school. They note the perfect grades on all that is attempted at school. Yet, is there not more to learning than schoolwork? A head of schools may receive a parent's complaint that their child is not learning the "important stuff" in school. Listen to the parent. Listen to the parent's examples. What are the life skills taught in the accelerated classrooms?

Much of the time, this situation occurs when a teacher needs additional training in instructing the advanced learner. Professional development addresses these educational opportunities to teach self-discipline and study skills within the prescribed curriculum. The lessons are comprised of enrichment assignments, more differentiated group work, open-ended assignments and even individualized self-applications. These types of lessons require specialized training to be built effectively. The end result is a rigorous and more significant experience for the gifted student.

The parent may consider accelerating their student into a different classroom. The choices for acceleration include skipping a grade level or a subject in a course progression, among other opportunities. It is wise to concentrate on what a child is learning. Study skills and self-discipline are applied to content and expectations that require more attention from the student. These more complicated exercises stretch the advanced learner into reaching their top learning capacity. Yet, be cognizant of the dialogue which will come home with the student. It is not "too difficult." The content just needs more of the student's cognitive abilities than prior academic classrooms.

Learning how to learn.

The advanced learner is the product of their past learning experiences. A student could have received perfect marks in elementary school without completing much homework and simply listened in class. High achieving students become experts at minimally preparing for an assessment, taking the assessment and promptly forgetting the material. Truly learning the material includes an ability to draw from the long-term memory to apply the learned principles or content to future problems. This method of minimal learning will drastically change when the student is placed in the proper challenging learning environment that fits their academic needs. This can be a difficult situation for both the student and the parent.

These situations arrive in the school leader's office at the beginning of each school year. This occurs most often when a child enters a new learning environment. This could be an accelerated elementary classroom, or the beginning of middle school and the beginning of high school. The child has always received high marks. What is wrong with the teachers in this new school? These words are sincere and correct. The teaching is different. The school leader or new teacher's role is to explain how the increased rigor is what the student needs to stretch their learning. A school leader who has spent time in the teacher's classroom will share relevant examples with the concerned parents.

A teacher who is organized and outlines specific expectations for all assignments and class agendas will eventually have parental support.

> ***Parent of high achiever to school leader:*** *I need to let you know that one of your teachers is not teaching our kids properly. My Sammy has not earned a "B" in his life. This sixth-grade science teacher gave him a "B." He studies all the time. He locks himself in his room for hours each night and studies. The tests must not be written correctly. I watch him study and he fails the tests!*
>
> ***School leader to concerned parent:*** *Let's talk about studying. Try asking Sammy to explain to you what he just learned from the book. See if he can accurately tell you the vocabulary applications and the content. Take it slow and enjoy the content together. This will help him move from "studying" to "learning" the material. This may take practice between the two of you. But stick with it and let me know how he is doing in the class.*

The parent will witness the student "studying" as in previous grades. It is important to note that "studying" is not the same as "learning." New skills are needed to meet the expectations in a rigorous learning environment. For example, if a student has the ability to teach what they just learned to a parent, they know the material. Try this with the child who is entering a new learning environment. The parent can request that the child to teach them what they learned after they read a chapter for homework. If the child knows the material, the parent will see it in how the child confidently teaches the material. This is an application of knowledge. It may not include the higher order thinking skills such as evaluation and analysis.

The curriculum's expectation of knowledge changes as students move into the higher secondary grades. Most state's accelerated curriculum programs, such as Advanced Placement, have a material requirement. Unfortunately, there is frequently not enough time to cover all the course material in class. The teacher provides readings and additional resources for students to explore and learn. The student is responsible for learning the new material on their own prior to the final summative assessment.

Frog Pond Theory: The student will try only until they are at the top of the class.

One of the most important questions a parent can ask is if their child is in the correct class for their learning level. As expressed in previous chapters, the group of students in a classroom has an effect on learning. The Frog Pond Theory provides an illustration of the many different children inside a classroom, or frog pond. The class is mixed with students of different learning abilities. They may all be identified as gifted students. Or, the students may be in differentiated classrooms with gifted and non-gifted students.

This theory expresses how learning occurs with the brightest student in the frog pond. Place this student in a class of middle and lower level learners and the advanced student will only try for the top of the class—no more—just the top. This translates into the top learner in an average or below average class. So, the high achiever is at the top of the average scale. The theory indicates this student will not proceed with their learning above their place as the top student on the average scale. They have won the top prize and stop to relish in their own brilliance.

Conversely, place the advanced student into a class of high achievers and the same Frog Pond Theory applies. The student works diligently for their place at the top of the class. The competitive student pushes toward the top of the class. This exercise pushes them close to or above the top learner in the class. The theory indicates the child who is placed in the average level class will only try to be the top average student. The same student placed in the accelerated classroom will try to be the top highest student.

It is important to note that the classroom is a social petri dish of human experiences. Each student knows the level of intelligence and grades of their peers. This knowledge is not provided by the teacher. It is acquired by competitive students. The exchanges between competitive students are not always kind.

The school leader and the teachers capitalize on the Frog Pond Theory with purposeful scheduling of students. Consider the gifted student's preference to not be placed into an accelerated classroom. They are aware of the dynamics and may prefer to avoid the intense competition. The average course may be more appealing. This situation calls for the school's leader to gather the counselor, gifted specialist, parents and teachers to discern what is the correct placement. All variables in the child's life are considered. The competitive class may be the obvious fit for the child's intelligence. However, a lesser course may be what the child needs during a difficult personal time.

Reading Discussion Activities

1. What is your opinion on the suggestion that a gifted student should "find their people?" What are the negative and positive aspects of this suggestion?
2. Think of a student you know who an under-achiever may be. Using the tools in this chapter and your own experiences, explain how you would advocate for this student.
3. How can your school help all teachers understand the elements of this chapter when creating lessons for all levels of learners?
4. How can your school help all parents of high achieving students understand the elements of this chapter?

Chapter 17
Are These Behaviors a Concern?

The advocates of the advanced learner know these students experience unique behaviors. These behaviors are common for some students and never experienced by others. At first glance an uninformed advocate may consider these behaviors as signs of low academic ability or laziness. The opposite is true: these behaviors are indicators of a highly intelligent student. These abbreviated descriptions provide the school leader a starting point in the understanding of the process of meeting the needs of these unique students.

These behaviors are described from a school leader's experiences. These are not descriptions from a licensed behavioral clinician. It is important to note that students who experience behaviors that pervasively and negatively affect their lives should be provided with professional assistance.

Perfectionists

The reasons the gifted learner is frequently a perfectionist is beyond the scope of this book. However, this personality trait is addressed due to its impact on the child, parent and school. Parents of perfectionists have felt the celebrations and emotional breakdowns of their children. This is a tight rope. Everyone wants their child to try their best. Perfectionism becomes an emotional crisis when a child makes impossibly high expectations or standards for their own accomplishments.

Part of the education process is to teach a child how to handle their own failures (or perceived failures). High achieving students have an expectation of their own successes. When confronted with activities or expectations which are unfamiliar, an imposter syndrome may arise in their emotional sensibilities. This syndrome relates to the student's self-image and may be reduced with positive mentorships and encouraging support.[1] Parents are aware of how their child makes choices following a less-than-perfect performance. These are learning moments for any age of child to build their self-esteem through encouragement.

Perfectionistic behavior is judged as both a negative and positive trait. There are two types of perfectionism: normal and neurotic.[2] The advanced learner has the potential of having both types. A normal perfectionist will receive edification from organized success and is motivated to put forth great effort to achieve established goals. Failure is shaken off and they move forward. The neurotic perfectionist sees errors in even the most brilliant work. They take their failures personally and hold them close for a long time.

Parents who are alert to the two types are wise to notice if the behaviors are healthy or dysfunctional. Expect the healthy perfectionists to seek out organization, support systems, and make personal efforts to meet their own high expectations. These gifted students are likely to have held the qualities of being responsible, accommodating, organized and considerate since a young age. Parents should intervene if their child acquires perfectionist behavior and is showing overt anxiety over perceived parental expectations, criticisms or even a fixation on not making mistakes.

The parent of a perfectionist child can assist in their management of this behavior by encouraging them to communicate their anxieties. This activity starts with trust between the child and the parent. Parents need to show their children when they make a mistake and model how to recover.

Criticism is especially difficult for all ages of young people and is to be avoided. Encourage the child in their strengths and never criticize or make fun of their appearance or what they value as important. Fostering a secure sense of self has a positive impact on the young gifted mind. Also, a little respectful humor about any situation relieves pressure and helps a student put their current "crisis" into perspective.

As a school leader, the perfectionist student bubbles up in parent conversations, student conferences and when a crisis is occurring. When counseling parents and children, keep an eye out for the two types of perfectionism. Encourage parents to take positive actions toward helping their child maintain healthy and productive perfectionate behaviors.

Procrastinators

School leaders may have their own issues with procrastinating staff members. Or, they may personally do their best work when under deadline pressures. Mentoring students by providing personal strategies during conferences is always a good method of relating to a student.

High level learners put the "pro" in procrastination. There are many assumptions as to why bright students wait until the last moment to complete their responsibilities. This is almost "normal" for the gifted student. This "normalcy" rarely makes the worried parent feel better about their child's condition.

One assumption is that students have much on their plates. Their list of tasks is long, and every item is important. By waiting until the due date is critically close, the student is required to prioritize their time. The student is forced to focus their intellectual energy on that one item. This does not work for all students. Or This does work for some students. But it drives their parents crazy as the different items on the priority list stack up against common deadlines.

Again, parents can model non-procrastination behaviors by communicating how they set daily goals on tasks with future deadlines. Do not let the little procrastinator hold the family hostage. Go on with the daily schedule. Allow the student to feel the pressure they created as part of their learning process. Promote strategies such as writing down a short list of daily goals each morning, posting calendars, crossing off completed tasks, celebrating early completions, etc.

Chronic Over-thinkers

A frequent parental complaint or description of their gifted children is their child's inability to take a situation or problem at face-value and move on to another topic. This analysis paralysis is common with students who enjoy analytical exercises. The problem arises when the student remains engrossed in the current analysis and has difficulty removing their mind from the analysis.

Parents are alerted to the "over thinker mindset" when their child is drawn to layers of thought unlike their peers. These over-thinkers seem to analyze all aspects of their world, predict problems, and see the trees and not the forest in most situations. The supportive parent is present and eases their child into an understanding that it is acceptable to move on or, it is acceptable to just look at the surface of the situation.

Redirecting their energy is a strategy to help students who tend to over think situations. Encourage them to turn their attention to a topic or activity that they enjoy and is somewhat temporary. This gives the student an escape from the situation that they may not be able to control and into a safe and happy situation. Light work such as exercising or working on a hobby frequently helps the over-thinker cope. Like any other habit, the over thinking student will find relief once they are aware of their thought processes and work to overcome it.

The Unorganized

The gifted student has the capacity to have all of these characteristics. In general, the student will exhibit one or all of these characteristics more often than other students. The advanced learner frequently experiences fast paced thoughts, and what appears to be random actions. The most effective accelerated classroom is designed to provoke original thoughts. The students are encouraged to work in groups to discover the lesson objectives. Teachers are encouraged to set up open learning through less structured lesson planning. This type of classroom is frequently viewed as noisy and unorganized.

These executive functioning skills may lag behind other developmental skills. It is not uncommon for a high level learner to struggle with what is perceived by others as a small task. A child's self-perception and happiness are not only dependent on raw intelligence, but also on their ability to successfully complete tasks and work through processes. Poor executive functioning skills can be a motivation killer. It is critical to listen, notice and support their learning through these perceived deficits.[3]

The professionally trained teacher in the gifted classroom creates this intellectual energy. They expertly provide the require tools to facilitate this type of learning. These organization tools enable the gifted learner to achieve their full potential. These tools are learned and repeatedly practiced. The gifted student will not always see the value of such practice. This rebellion is often labeled as unorganized.

Parents are an integral part in the development of a child's organized mindset. Their modeling and communication of their own organization strategies provides a foundation in first grade and beyond. It is recommended to provide a child with a paper agenda and practice using it. The agenda aids in the recording and predictability of assignments. This becomes a habit, or an obsession, to write everything down.

Middle School Teacher Scenario: *We have had the same notebook structure in grades 6 through 8 for over ten years. The students learn the system in the first weeks of 6th grade. They apply this organization system throughout middle school. Students who enter the school in the 7th or 8th grade are given an abbreviated tutorial on the notebook. Most students take these skills with them to high school and even college. However, some parents want to create their own system. I understand they want to help their child, but this upsets our binder organization procedures. I tell them that we do not use folders and to trust us that this system works. Most of the parents get it and help us encourage our most unorganized child to stay with the binder system.*

The unorganized student thrives on predictable routines. These routines are set up at home as well as school. Regardless of age, a student needs to set a time for their wake-up, homework, binder organization dinner, bedtime and other important routines. This dependable structure helps maintain consistent habits.

Organization takes time and patience from the student, parent and teacher. These are life skills that are even a struggle for adults. As a child ages into secondary grades, these agendas and daily routines provide a foundation to keep track of expectations. Their classes become more complex with seasons of assignments and assessments. A good organization system is one of the pillars of success in accelerated academics.

Isolation by Choice

No, it is not acceptable for a child of any age to spend hours alone. In most cases, this is the choice of the child. It takes an alert, resourceful and strong-minded parent to break this cycle of isolation. Remember, the bright child is aware of their parent's habits and parenting skills. Even at a very young age, a gifted child has the ability to predict parental behaviors. When entering the gifted child's world to make a correction, know that they are one step ahead of the parent's argument for change. They will use this knowledge to counter the request to exit their familiar situation.

Parent Scenario: *I am so glad the school holds a "Honors Students Dance." I never heard of this type of dance before we started at this middle school. At first, Billy said there was no way he would go to a dance. I insisted by telling him this may be his only dance experience in school. He attended and knew everyone at the dance. And, to make it even better, the school had all sorts of games. It was more of a "social" than a dance. Not very many students danced but they all played the games. That was three weeks ago, and he is still talking about it.*

The child's school has a plethora of opportunities to engage a child in activities with similar students. Parents are encouraged to communicate with the school leader or counselor regarding extra-curricular activities. The student's friends or potential friends are good sources for activities. Start slow and gently encourage interaction.

Reading Discussion Activities

1. Explain how the school and their support team of specialists address unwanted or concerning behaviors. Give positive and negative examples.
2. Discuss specific children you have experienced with these behavior characteristics. What actions can be taken to help these students?
3. Brainstorm possible trainings for school staff and parents which address these issues in the classroom, the school and at home.

Chapter 18
The Unique Social and Emotional Needs of an Advanced Learner

The social and emotional needs of a high achiever are important to consider when making decisions for them or when changing their life's routine. As expressed in prior sections, students of all learning levels are the most comfortable when they find "their people." However, there are caveats to this practice. A class of high achievers will relate to each other's abilities to successfully navigate the school's expectations to receive high grades. But, is that where the similarities end?

The identification process impacts student social structures

Early identification of giftedness occurs during the student's elementary years. These students are aware of who "made it" and who did not earn the *gifted* status. This knowledge creates a relational grouping of students with similar characteristics. The students, teachers and even the school separates these students by their label. The social and emotional questions arise with this process. What if the student's closest friends are not gifted? What if the recently labeled student does not identify with, or like, the other gifted students? What if the newly identified gifted student is not welcomed by the other gifted students.

***Parent and School Counselor:** I remember when I was tested for gifted in elementary school. I didn't want to be in the gifted program because my peers who were in the program were always pulled out of class and I didn't want to leave my friends in class to go to 'gifted class'. I actually remember purposefully answering questions incorrectly so that I didn't qualify.*

The school leader and their staff have the ability to monitor and take positive actions in making this transition into a gifted program more palatable for newly identified students. First, communication takes place between the student's teachers, the counselor and parents. In this circle, the child has the opportunity to voice their concerns. A program is provided for the student that aligns with their best interests while meeting the requirements to accelerate learning.

Identification of giftedness in the secondary school years can be less emotional than the elementary identification process due to the manner by which classes are scheduled. In general, the classes are separated by subject. A recently identified gifted student is placed in an accelerated class instead of an average class. The beginning of a school year is the preferred time to select courses designed with higher rigor.

Gifted groupings: Identifiable Characteristics

The cohorts of students identified as gifted have their own functioning personalities. These students are competitive with each other. Grades for assignments, tests and final grades are widely known by the group. The students share this confidential information. Each student in their cluster groupings know where they fall on the grade spectrum. This competitive element is balanced into two extremes. The child who needs to study to keep their place in the group is motivated to learn. The child who drops down into the lower quartile of the group feels ostracized or judged by their peers.

The student who has always been the "smart kid" in elementary school is mixed with other "smart kids" from multiple schools upon entering 6th grade. This phenomenon also occurs at the high school level. This is a powerful reckoning for the student. Their reaction follows their need to fit in or to excel above the others.

A proactive school staff responds to theses social and emotional needs of students in the first few weeks of classes in the new school. Parents and students will notice the student's change in behavior during the first quarter of class. A meeting with the student, counselor, teachers, parents and school administrator is critical during this time of adjustment. It is in this confidential circle that the student can voice their opinion of the new school, the other students, the teachers, etc. Everyone at the table wants the student to succeed in school. The student receives learning tools and encouraging conversations to make it through these adjustments.

Principal's conversation with a future high school freshman: *The student waited with his father to speak with me during our lively Freshman Orientation. He was a tall boy and his father stood back behind him. The young man introduced himself and let me know his current middle school grade point average. I asked him why he was interested in attending my school for high academics. He puffed up and claimed his top position in the 8th grade. He assertively announced his intention to earn the valedictorian of his senior class at graduation. That was four years ago. Nick and I spoke almost daily during his tenure at my high school. He and I worked through some growing pains. He was always truthful and ready to listen to the "adult" side of an issue, although he did not always agree. And, yes, he was the valedictorian. His claim to me after gaining acceptance to Columbia was to cure childhood leukemia. This amazing young man has held true to his claim to be valedictorian of a highly competitive school. Without nurturing him through these four formative years his abilities may not be up to curing childhood leukemia. Now, he has a great start. He may do just that.*

This scenario is an illustration of how newcomers enter a group of gifted students. This competitive nature is real. There are other students who are not as competitive and simply enjoy the higher academic rigor. Parents and school leaders need to be keenly aware of how this dynamic occurs within the school. The segregation process starts early in the school year. Parents are advised to keep an open communication with their child and other parents. School leaders will orchestrate community building activities with new students. School counselors will schedule many conferences where all attendees will be heard in building a program for the student.

Notably, the veteran teacher of high achieving students is an expert on the social and emotional issues which effect their gifted students. Listen to their assessments of the student's needs. Know that they are on the front line to make a child feel comfortable, smart, and most importantly, a welcome part of their cohort. Parents are wise to realize the limited time of their child's teacher. A simple positive and short nudge through email or a positively worded card establishes a partnership with the teacher.

Reasonable Balance: Growing Pains or Too Much Pressure?

Children are not smaller versions of adults. They feel life differently. Their pressures are real to them. Their communication skills are not developed. In many situations, it is easier for them to not speak than to engage with adults. Parents and all who advocate for the gifted student realize these idiosyncrasies. A passion for learning and reason exists along with the childlike or adolescent mind.

It is acceptable and encouraged to celebrate a child's differences and unique abilities to conquer the academic world. Yet, young minds require a balance in the child's world to function. Watch as they grow exponentially under the careful watch of their advocates who understand their need to expand into social situations.

School provides young intellectuals with a safe place to compare their strengths to others. As mentioned in previous chapters, gifted students need to be active in the school environment. A sport or civic club allows the student to explore their non-academic strengths. This development has the potential to stress the young mind as they stretch outside their comfort zones. A supportive family structure and good friends nurture this balance.

Father speaks out at the freshman parent meeting held in mid-September: *You have taken my daughter away from me. She used to sit with the family at dinner. Now, she is in her room studying. I mean, really studying. She does not want to go out during the weekend because of her homework. I want my daughter back. Your school asks too much of these kids. Let them be kids.*

Parents may notice as a child enters higher grade levels that their ability to grasp concepts and complete homework with past efficiency is compromised. The exposure to higher and more rigorous expectations stretches the young scholars. They need to find their balance in the learning and application of new material. The secondary scholar is not the same type of learner as the elementary scholar. The student is maturing into the adult scholar role. Parents will notice this shift in less time spent on activities outside of academics. The balance will return. The student is "learning how to learn." This adapting to more rigorous expectations takes time to master.

My parents won't notice… the "A" Student Syndrome

In general, the parents of gifted students do not need to intervene in the school environment to ensure their child's success. Students find their own way as a result of their own motivations to work diligently on their schoolwork. They have good grades. Parent conferences are rare and school discipline issues tend to be non-existent.

Parents of students who are "off the radar" are advised to keep an active eye on their child's mood and routine. Changes in an attitude, friend groups and routine indicate a change in their school or home environment. A higher maintenance sibling will take the focus off the sibling with the high grades and no behavior issues. The needs of this child are less obvious. Compliance is not to be interpreted as the child not needing parental attention, support and interactions.

Privacy in a home is the parent's option. The parameters are set by the parents for the safety and well-being of their child. Remember, highly intelligent students have the capacity to predict their parent's behaviors. Listening to a child must be companioned with discerning their intentions in what they truly mean to say or are not saying.

Sue Klebold, mother of gifted Columbine High School shooter, Dylan Klebold, to Diane Sawyer on ABC News' 2020: *"I felt that I was a good mom … that he would, he could talk to me about anything. Part of the shock of this was learning that what I believed and how I lived and how I parented was an invention in my own mind. That it, it was a completely different world that he was living in."*[2]

Teachers alert school leaders and parents of a change in a child's behavior. Listen to these advocates. Veteran teachers are experts in child behaviors. They are a resource for parents. A parent who utilizes this resource learns more about their child. An open dialogue between a teacher and the student's parents has the capacity to build a strong foundation for the child's future successes.

Work Ethic and the Development of Self-Efficacy

The critical calendar months for the students in a rigorous academic program are August, October, and December. Underachievement is not the problem but a symptom.[2] The first month in classes provides the student with the expectations and the need to hit the ground running on assignment expectations. It is their choice to do the work to get the grades.

By the end of the first quarter of the school year, the child realizes their strengths and weaknesses in successfully completing a rigorous academic program. Friends and family members are expecting the same habits from the student. The student is realizing they must give up their previous free time and replace it with academics. This is where the "rubber meets the road." It is the student's choice to make these changes.

By the end of the first semester, the successful student is in a rhythm of time management. The student who has not achieved in their classes will experience heightened anxiety. This anxiety emerges from a self-awareness of what it takes to succeed and their inability or unwillingness to meet the new standard. Their self-efficacy plummets as their circle of supporters question the student's abilities.

Math teacher during a teacher/student conference with failing student: *Eric, when you first came to our Algebra 2 class at the beginning of 9th grade, you had a different attitude. It was obvious you had friends in the class from your gifted math class in middle school. Here we are in October, and you have stopped trying. I know you can do this work. You are so smart. (Eric mumbles)*

Eric's mom: *Look, Eric wants out of this Algebra 2 honors class. He says it takes him too long to do his homework. I want my kid well-rounded and he has other interests outside of school. Like gaming. He is gaming with people all over the world. He has always gotten good grades. He wants out.*

Math teacher looking at Eric: *So, I now know why you want out of this class. You want to spend more time on your video games.*

Does the student's work ethic match their giftedness? It is important to repeat that the willingness to adapt to challenges is the student's choice. Do they want to produce? These are social and emotional questions addressed by the school, counselors, teachers and parents. Listen and watch for their messages on what the student wants.

Cheaters and Liars:

The pressure of performing at the top of a student's ability scale at all times is intense. The tenacity to keep this momentum impacts the social and emotional well-being of any student. Add the competitive nature of the high achiever with peer pressures and a short cut looks enticing.

It is important that cheating is addressed often and outwardly in advanced learner programs. Students choose to take the easy way to "get the A" by purposefully cheating. Teachers are responsible for designing assignments that make it difficult for students to cheat.

However, the option to cheat is present in every assignment. A teacher needs the support of the school leader when they tell a parent that their child cheated. This is often a first occurrence for the parent. The teacher needs to have evidence of the offense.

Yes, it still counts as cheating if you don't get caught!

Consequences for cheating must meet the offense and the gifted student's currency. These consequences capitalize on the student's competitive nature and are personally intense for a young scholar. They set an early precedence that cheating is a serious offense. The list below reflects the school leader's knowledge of the competitive gifted learner in determining the consequences for each offender.

A Gifted-Relevant School Consequence Plan for Cheating

First Offense

1. The child receives a zero on the course work on which they cheated.
2. The child who shared the course work receives a zero for their work.
3. The child's teacher communicates the offense and the consequences with all the other teachers who have these children in the school.
4. The school administrator and counselor are informed.
5. The student's parents are informed with a telephone call or in-person visit.
6. The first offense is above.

Second Offense

7. Suspension from school.

It is advisable for all students, regardless of age, and their parents to sign a Behavior Contract at the beginning of each school year. The behavior expectations and consequences are listed in this contract and in school assemblies.

There are multiple reasons why a student speaks untruths to their parents and others in their social circle. Lying is frequently a symptom of a deeper issue and needs a thorough analysis each time it occurs. As with adults, a child who lies is either seeking a response or avoiding a response. Consequences and the questioning of the intent of the lying must be addressed with each occurrence.

These are a few examples of how a lie is a deeper symptom of a child's thoughts. Lying is often an attention seeking behavior in a world where everyone is going in separate directions and the compliant gifted child is frequently overlooked. The perfectionist lies to keep their self-imposed high level of outcomes in their lives. Take the time to listen to their reasons for the lie and carefully discern corrective actions.

Veteran school leaders recognize a lie and take action to learn more about the student's reason for this offense. These are common occurrences in a school. As the student explains their reasoning for the untruth, the school staff is alerted to the emotional and social needs of the student. This form of advocacy for the gifted student builds a trust in future interactions.

When are Expectations too High?

The leaders of schools have the opportunity to get to know students over several years. Their constant presence and encouragement resonate throughout the school culture. It is the responsibility of the school leader and their staff to recognize the needs of all levels of learners. A keen eye will notice if a child is not themselves by a change in their behavior or routine.

The social and emotional needs of the advanced learner will bubble up and show themselves to the adult who cares to notice. Parents are on the front line and will use their nurturing skills to discern their child's needs. They are charged with taking notice, then taking action.

Accelerated programs demand the time and attention of each student. Parents and other student advocates "read the room" for anomalies where students are learning. A parent may watch their student study for hours, yet the grades do not indicate learning has occurred. Remember, "studying" is different from "learning." Helpful tips on learning course material and other resources is available from teachers. Strategies such as asking the child to teach the material to a parent are recommended.

Students choose to be with "their people." Notice if the student's friends are not in their classes for advanced learners. Longtime friends are an exception. However, new friends who are not in their classes are a sign of separation from their academic peers. Talk to the child about this separation and listen to their response. It may be simply that these peers have lower expectations of the child. The gifted student may be weary of competing with upper scholars. Be vigilant in recognizing if bullying is occurring in the accelerated courses. These are just a few examples of how a change in behavior is the result of a social or emotional reaction.

Students identified as gifted may choose to stop trying to succeed for many reasons as expressed in these chapters. The students are experts at self-sabotage. The parental and school advocates have no weapon which will combat a child who self-sabotages their grades. Of course, all advocates will try to "get the student back on track" with incentives and punishments. Listen to the student and know their desires. If a student wants out of an accelerated program, they will make it so.

> ***Parent's discussion with school administration:*** *I know Kristin is not identified as gifted. She missed the cut-off score when she was in second grade. She really wants to stay with her friends in her new middle school. Please place her in the advanced classes. She told me she wants to work hard to stay in these classes with her friends from elementary school. I can tell she means it. I know this is not your regular procedure for placing students in the advanced classes. But, please give her a chance.*

Conversely, the student who wants into an accelerated program without the gifted identification has the motivation to succeed. Students who want to work on advanced academics in their preferred subject find strategies to learn the material. These social and emotional journeys are apparent if the adults notice the actions of the student. Be aware of the students' actions and listen to their voices.

The social and emotional journey of a struggling gifted student

The mental well-being of students is often cloaked in an attempt to fit in with students who are seemingly succeeding. This ability for students to hide their anxiety creates a growing burden on a student's ability to cope. These pressures arise from their own high expectations of themselves, parental and peer pressure. They have never been lower than the top of their class. The Smart Kid status is their identification. The student's advocates grasp at strategies to heal the student.

School leaders are not usually experts in pediatric mental health. Partnering with student-centered mental health experts is the first step to understanding how to implement positive programs in a school. The experts have a list of "wants" to serve students who need their services. It is left to the school's administration to find the funds, space and personnel to meet their students' social and emotional needs.

Indicators of a student's happiness and life satisfaction are radiating positive emotions. Building blocks of well-being are noticed in their gratitude, empathy and overall positive nature. The child's basic needs seem to be met through their home, school and community life. Students with a positive social and emotional spirit have strong social relationships with friends or family. Their social and emotional communications match their age level. When asked, they can communicate their interpretation of their support systems, healthy interactions, minimal bullying and a safe, nurturing environment.

Negative indicators of mental health are frequently noticeable to the child's advocates in the home and school. These children will internalize their problems which may manifest in their anxiety and depression. Investigation into the causes look for trauma and other environmental stressors. Advocates may notice behavior changes in the withdrawal from previously enjoyed activities and cognitive lapses. Disruptive behaviors will include deviance from the rules which were previously important to the student. It is important to keep consistent rules and expectations in the student's life. This will help discern any risky or unsafe situations.

> ***High School Counselor:*** *As a counselor, the students I met with who were doing self-harm or considering harming themselves, were almost always the high achieving students. These students tend to be anxious and they put a ton of pressure on themselves to be perfect.*

The knowledgeable mental health professional provides guidelines for the school leaders and counselors to follow when working with an at-risk student. A risk assessment is taken and generally involves whether a student has a plan and opportunity to hurt themselves or others. Is there a precipitating event? History of behavior or patterns? Parents and school staff are advised to seek the advice of mental health professional when concerned for a child's safety.

Parents have the power to create an opportunity for their child to thrive in their home. Listed are a few tips in creating a home environment that enhances positive mental health:

1. Create a predictable home environment.
2. Keep consistent expectations for each family member.
3. Create and keep family routines.
4. Create and keep consistent times for homework, bedtime and meals.
5. Make sure the environment is not overstimulating.
6. Be mindful of the order of the environment. Less busy or cluttered environments give space for cognitive energy.
7. Listen to the children's concerns. Patiently interpret their meanings.
8. Walk through a future potentially upsetting event with the child. These clear steps provide predictability and avoid emotional surprises.

School leaders play an active and important role in creating positive mental health environments for their students and their staff. Professional development for all staff in the recognizing of potential mental health issues is critical. Students are wholly supported if all adults in their life have the knowledge and ability to notice an issue. An alert and well-trained staff will notice social and academic shifts in students. Schools have the capacity to help students succeed despite any adverse childhood experiences at home.

Reading Discussion Activities

1. As a parent, what is your expectation of school leaders? Be specific, write a list.
2. Write down 3 – 5 comments regarding parent questions or concerns that are heard each school year. Then write a solution for these concerns. Include what is in the power of the school administration, school counselor, teachers, parents, etc.
3. As a parent, school leader, counselor, teacher, etc. discuss the high achieving student and mental health issues. Relate their situation. Indicate what is needed to provide support.

Chapter 19
A Parent's Role in their Gifted Child's School:
Caveats and Accolades

The nation's landscape in serving gifted students is where a parent starts on a path to advocate for their child. There are few state regulations and fewer federal policies governing gifted education. The result of a lack of accountability is the unequal distribution of gifted services in schools. School districts work diligently to meet the exceptional needs of all students. Yet, the students identified as gifted often stay off the resource allocation spreadsheets due to their predicted ability to graduate from high school.

Furthermore, underserved populations of students are less identified than other students. Poverty is a key factor in this lack of identification. Cognitive tests and teacher and parental referrals still rule student access to gifted screening. Universal screening of all students at specific grade levels positively impacts the process but is rarely considered due to the scarcity of resources.

A parent should be concerned if their gifted student starts a school year ahead of non-gifted students in reading and mathematics achievement yet does not excel at a quicker pace than their peers. This lack of acceleration is a result of the inappropriate application of gifted education strategies. In general, teachers assigned to teach gifted education select their curriculum and pacing. Professional training in gifted education with follow ups on instructional outcomes is critical to effective acceleration.

School leaders face these issues and more in their quest to meet the needs of each level of learner in their school. Resources are systemically a factor. A savvy administrator listens to their staff and experts in gifted education. They communicate which resources are needed. The school is responsible for procuring these resources.

Is Gifted Education the Right Fit?

Some parents arrive at a school with an affirmed belief that their child is unusually bright. Does the school see the same child? A systematic referral process and identification screenings are in place to cull out the gifted students in early grades and beyond. This is usually an internal school district procedure which the school leaders follow through their gifted specialists or other exerts on assessments. Gifted students will sometimes express an interest to be withdrawn from these specialized pullouts or accelerated classrooms. The student has the power to work to excel or sabotage this pathway. In the end, the student will be placed in the classroom where they desire.

> ***Parent to school administrator:*** *I thank you for taking my calls and setting up the past three conferences. Your teachers are difficult! Shaniqua did fine in elementary school in these gifted classes. I appreciated what your teachers said to me about her abilities and that was not why she was not trying. We will get to the bottom of why she does not want to be in the gifted classes. I thought we could convince her, but she kept destroying her schoolwork. Well, she won. Two nights ago, she stopped eating. I am serious. This is her ultimate power play. Her dad, and I gave in. Please change her schedule.*

Parents must decide their next step if their child is not identified as gifted. Should they push or not push for more screening? The answer is in the motivation for the labeling of the student. Will the student have access to upper level courses? The administrator has the ability to wave this requirement. Will the student be placed into classes with their friends? Again, the administrator has the ability to place students into specific classes. Will the student receive access to any other program or club which is specifically designed for the identified gifted student? The same answer applies. Work with the school leaders to advocate for a non-gifted, yet motivated child.

Advocating for a student can take a sensitive path. It takes a bold advocate to break down barriers within a system. Pleasant persistence coupled with knowledge and solutions bring positive results. Consider these tips from Dr. Harold S. Koplewicz, MD[1] for making school personnel an ally:

- ❍ **Communicate with your child and ask questions.** A warm positive relationship with care takers generates a happy child. Keep positive and let the student speak their mind without correction.
- ❍ **Recognize that your child behaves differently at home and school.** Teachers have a sense of a child's emotional and cognitive abilities. Feel comfortable asking about strengths and weaknesses. Be careful not to have a "blaming tone."
- ❍ **Maximize parent-teacher conference time.** Write out specific questions and ask them at the beginning of the conference. Feel confident to lead the meeting.
- ❍ **Don't delay getting support for your child.** Regularly scheduled Parent-Teacher conferences may be infrequent. Ask to meet and provide convenient dates for all team members.
- ❍ **Request special services in writing.** Keep everything in writing. Evaluations are conducted at no cost, but most requests must be in writing. Ask for copies of student records.
- ❍ **Meet with the people who evaluate your child.** The written results do not include the affective parts of the evaluations. The evaluator will clarify the process and results.
- ❍ **Understand the Individual Education Plan or Education Plan.** Parents are part of the team that creates these plans. Speak up.
- ❍ **Monitor your child's moods.** Trust your intuition when behavior shifts.

(Adapted from Dr. Harold S. Koplewicz's Child Mind Institute)

A parent is often the first to notice their child's unique cognitive abilities. These high aptitude traits become more evident as the child matures. Keep a portfolio with the specific milestones and growth. These aspects of acuity are important as the child develops. List awards and successes in extracurricular activities. If a gifted program is not accessible in the child's school, the parent has vast options of non-school based activities for enrichment. Family travel and reading together is enriching. Enroll students in community programs, such as scouting, intermural sports, technology camps, etc.

The student who is identified through a recent screening and evaluation may have a choice of when to be enrolled into gifted classes. The student may prefer to enter the courses at the beginning of the next school year. This is a choice with social impacts. Only the student fully understands the ramifications of this schedule change. This is also the choice of the child and parent. The newly identified student will have an opinion on their placement. A school's policy to immediately enter the student is just that: a school policy. The school leader has the power to override the policy at the parent's request.

The Consideration of Acceleration Options

If a student is high functioning, then they need a place in their school where they can excel to the top of their abilities. Not all acceleration options fit every student. With advice from the school experts and the child's input, parents have the power to select their child's acceleration options. Their child's motivation and attitude toward learning is essential in finding the correct placement. When gifted students are accelerated, there is an increase in academic achievement.[2]

The school leader's responsibility is to sift through the accelerated conversations and determine the student's choice. The administrators have the power to serve the students who fall outside the set guidelines others may be required to follow. Parents advocate for their child by expressing their preferred acceleration.

The age and grade level of the student is an indicator of how to place the student appropriately. Consider the nine-year-old who can master Algebra 2 in a high school classroom. This does not signify this is the proper placement. The student's social and emotional needs come into play. A solution is to match their cognitive abilities with advanced curriculum in their current school. Additionally, students who are small in stature will stand out in a class of older students. Skipping grades is advisable only if the situation enhances the child's education. Other options are online math courses, a self-paced independent study or other course delivery models which keep the student with their age group while accelerating in one course. All elements of this decision are under consideration prior to the move to the next grade.

Skipping grade levels or courses in a set course progression in high school is much more palatable for the student. Moving from a 9th grade mathematics course to an 11th grade course is a smooth transition. Most of the students are of like physical stature. Plus, the advanced mathematic students tend to enjoy each other's brilliance. A young newcomer would most likely be academically challenged, then welcomed to their "club."

The ability of the child to quickly learn new material may not be challenged by skipping a grade. This temporary fix will be evident when the student simply excels beyond the upper level course or grade. It is preferable to advance the curriculum with self-directed or enrichment strategies built on the individual student's academic requirements. Acceleration is most fulfilling to the student when instruction and course content is tailored to the student's abilities.[3] There is a plethora of acceleration options which greatly vary in schools. Parents are advised to meet with the school leader, counselor and a gifted specialist on available options.

Gifted Specialist describing a recently identified student:
The parents told me they thought he was different. Kyle is only 14 years old. They noticed he was unique from other kids his age in his social interactions. After being identified as gifted, Kyle's parents expressed relief. They were grateful the school used a universal screening process for the 9th graders. The family has decided to accelerate Kyle during his 10th grade school year. It will be interesting to see how he adapts to his new classes. I am looking forward to helping him.

Acceleration of students who are twice exceptional takes additional information to ensure their academic success. The uneven needs are presented to the school staff by the parent to find solutions. For example, a student who scores high on academic achievement assessments, yet is woefully unorganized and has dastardly penmanship still needs advanced opportunities. The school has the responsibility of providing support for the student in their additional exceptionality. This is an expectation which is met by the school and active parental involvement in support of the student.

Ramifications of Not Accelerating

Making a decision to avoid acceleration has an impact on the student's future learning. A student who is not challenged is at risk for behavior and developmental problems. Bright students will not learn how to learn in classes that are not challenging. A student who wants to take the easiest path will not need to study to learn the course material. Their presence in a classroom is often the only requirement for success. This generates poor work habits and a loss of motivation to excel in any course. A combination of options to accelerate the student in multiple areas is advisable such as extracurricular programs, summer enrichments, etc. Parents and school staff work together to create individualized opportunities for the student.

The Student-Parent Conference: It Takes a Village. Listen to the Teachers!

The conference is called by any of the student's advocates: the parent, counselor, teacher or school leader. An effectively led conference centers on the student. Therefore, conferences are referred to as "student conferences" not "parent conferences." Frequently, these meetings are held to determine the reason for a breech in expectations. The main topic is generally based on student performance, but can also be centered around behaviors, peer relationships, home issues, etc. The school leader sets the tone of the conference with a student-centered culture.

Students know why they are earning their current grades. There is rarely a situation in which the student is in the dark about their grade.

The parent may hold the teacher or the teacher's system responsible for the student's grade. This meeting is when the student will expose the reason for the grade. Ask the student to explain in great detail the issue in the classroom. Lying will reveal itself during the explanation.

The school leader spends time in classrooms and is acutely aware of the teacher's classroom procedures. In general, it is a privilege to teach high achieving students. These teachers know the gifted student. There is a good chance they have heard these excuses in the past. Understand, some teachers have idiosyncrasies which negatively affect the student's progress. These conversations take place between the teacher and the administrator following the conference.

Student conference*: Joey is identified as gifted and was the top of his 8th grade class in a small rural school. He and his mom decided he should attend the accelerated high school. The school administration knew his academic abilities brought him to the school. He also knew the academics at the middle school were not rigorous. Joey earned his middle school grades easily without learning organizational skills or completing homework. He was proud to be the smartest kid in the class. But he was not the smartest in the large high school classes. His mom let him take a wrestling class his sophomore year. He fell in love with the sport. The conference concluded with Joey's transfer to regular classes and promising everyone he would be the wrestling star of the school. The advanced students were strangers to him. Joey found his "people" with the wresting team and his grades in the regular classes were exceptional.*

Be prepared to learn something new about the student. If the conference is set up correctly, the safe environment will generate honest discussions. The student takes the responsibility of explaining the reasons for their grades or behavior. The teachers enlighten the parent. If not, the parent can ask direct questions that cannot be answered by the teacher with a simple Yes or No. For example, please explain your expectations for how students are to hand in their homework when they enter class.

Attending a conference is similar to going to a medical doctor. Prepare questions ahead of time and ensure all concerns are addressed prior to exiting the conference. Watch the clock. Make sure the top concerns are addressed first. There is a limit on the number of minutes teachers, counselors, and administrators will stay at the table.

These are a simple set of questions parents or child advocates should ask during a conference. Each question is lead to more clarifying information shared by the team at the conference.[4]

1. How is my child doing socially and emotionally?
2. In which areas does my child need improvement?
3. Is my child giving their best effort?
4. Describe your teaching style.
5. How can I help at home?

A parent should refrain from asking for special favors from their child's teacher. For example, a parent insists the child finishes their homework and places it in their backpack. The parent requests that the teacher approach the child each day to ask for the homework in the backpack. This request is unacceptable in the educational process of the student who learns they own the responsibility for turning in their homework, not the teacher.

Reading Discussion Activities

1. Make a parallel list of the pluses and deltas of the reasons to accelerate, and not to, accelerate a student.
2. With your team, develop a template for student-parent conferences. Include the information from this chapter. This template serves as a guide for all conference participants: student, parent, teacher, counselor, specialist, administration, etc.
3. Consider how the parent of a gifted child sees the school. Give detailed descriptions through the parent's lens: of the support of high achieving children, acceleration information and options, experiences in a student-conference

CHAPTER 20
A Parent's Relationship with Schools and with Their Gifted Student

Concerned parents arrive at their child's school daily to advocate for their children. School staff understand their role is to respectfully serve parents. There is a culture or atmosphere in a school when the parent arrives. How are they greeted? Do they have access to the front office? The principal? Their child?

It is common for parents to arrive or communicate with a school when an issue has occurred. Other occurrences may involve the seeking of information from the persons who have specific information regarding the school or their child. Training on how to interact with an angry, agitated or otherwise unhappy person is critical for the school's front-line staff.

The school leader creates an expectation from their staff that all parents will be served as if they are the most important parent in the school. The parent arriving or calling the office asking for assistance is as unique as their child. Each parent is welcomed as if they were the only person in the school. Remember, their children are the most important people in their lives. They are advocating for their family.

Each School Culture Reflects Support for Advanced Learners

The culture of servicing parents, families, community and students comes from the top. Parents deciding on which school to send their child should make a quick trip into each school's front office. Ask the front office personnel a question (about gifted education) that is unique and requires their research or advocacy. The response will reveal the level of service. This is an indication of how the leadership supports parents.

A meeting with the school leader, parent leaders or teachers will reveal the school's philosophy on the education of the gifted student. Ask questions which require in depth knowledge of gifted education. If the school leader does not have the answer, who do they ask? If it is their gifted specialist or a teacher of the gifted, watch how they interact. Is there a respect for these experts?

The best environment a school leader can create is a school culture that goes above and beyond to serve the students identified as gifted. The achievements of advanced learners are obviously celebrated through accolades posted in the hallways, on websites, etc. The school leader should have examples of specific students who have earned notable competitive awards.

A parent understands the school's gifted culture through the allocation of the school's resources. Check out the student's schedules or the master schedule. Are high ability students allowed to spend time together in classes? If not, how does the school group their gifted students? The faculty reveals how the gifted are accelerated. These are short conversations because teachers usually have a pulse, and an opinion, on how students are served in the school. The parent is looking for an opinion on the quality of service. For example, asking more advanced students to tutor younger gifted students or assigning extra work is not an acceptable strategy to serve gifted students.

Best Practices for Advocating for a Student in Schools

An issue occurs and the parent needs action to take place in a school. The nature of the issue is irrelevant to the best practices to have it addressed within a school structure. The tips below are important to know prior to addressing a school.

- *Make an appointment, alert the favored secretary of your arrival. Find out if the meeting is possible prior to arriving.*

- Schools are busy institutions where "putting out fires" occurs daily as part of the routine. A parent in need is important. Yet, there are priorities to follow when a school sets up a student-centered culture.
- This calls for a parent's patience and productive communication. For example, it is not advised to arrive in the front office for an unexpected request to meet with the principal on the same day as a schoolwide assembly, visit from the school district leaders, following a lockdown, when an employee was transported to the hospital, when substitutes do not show up, a student has an immediate need, during lunches attended by the principal, or during a teacher's scheduled evaluation, etc.

❍ *Know who is in charge.*

- Find out if the person who is telling you "no" has the ability to provide the "yes." For example, teachers and gifted specialists have policies and procedures to follow. Depending on how the system is set up, they may have a student load of 10 to 100. Their job is to carry out the directives to meet requirements. They may not have the tenacity or the time to make exceptions to the rule. These changes in the routine take time and they do not have the time.
- The school's administrator may be the only person in the school who can override the directives to provide the "yes" to a parent's request. The school leader will need background reasons for the request, as they are probably not versed in gifted education. The student-centered school leader will listen and act on the best interest of the student. A "yes" decision from the school leader releases the previous person who said "no" from liability in the breaking of the policies or procedures.
- If the school's administrator will not grant the "yes," and the reasons are simply that it is policy, the parent needs to find the person who can grant the "yes." School leadership

is a political position. Many times, the school leaders would rather send a parent to their supervisors than take the responsibility of changing a policy. Ensure the request is possible.

- Know what you want.
  - If a parent can visualize exactly what they want from the school for their child, what does it look like? This exercise helps the parent see the what is important.
  - The different roadblocks to overcome to get to this end are not the focus. The focus is the visualized final result. For example, a parent wants to accelerate their 7th grade gifted child into an 8th grade math course. The school counselor and teacher say this is not what the school does because he would be left without a math in 8th grade. The parent's role is to get their child into the 8th grade math class during their 7th grade year. It is not the parent's role to find the next course to take in the 8th grade year. This is the responsibility of the school's leader and their staff. Additionally, never take a "no" because of a system-centered issue. Systems can be changed, altered, etc. The student-centered school will change the class and look for other 7th graders who may qualify.
  - Parents are asking for a longer road to the end goal if there is too much dialogue about the consideration of different options. By walking in with a viable solution, the conversation starts with the reason why this can or cannot be allowed. Parents should not ask the counselor, teacher, or school leader an open-ended question such as "how are you going to help my child?" Start the conversation with: I want, I need, make this specific change, etc.
- *Know the law*: Federal, state and district.
  - A few online searches of the laws that impact their child are a worthy of a parent's time. Look at the links in the first chapter and research the law. Know the law prior to asking for a change.

- Avoid using the law as a hammer, the laws function as protectors of children, their families and schools. Recite the laws that support the parent's request. If the school, district or other entity will still not budge, ask how they will meet the requirements of this law.

❍ What are parental rights?

- The rights of parents in schools is different based on their state. The 10th Amendment of the Constitution gave states the authority to write these rights into their state constitutions. A quick web search will reveal the parents' rights in their state. Check the "standards" at the "Your state" Department of Education. Furthermore, school districts have additional standards for schools to follow.
- The list below are highlights of five of the rights of parents and their children. The additional rights are best explored using specific events or issues which relate to the written federal, state or district laws.
  - **The right to a free education. Students** who attend a public school should not have to pay for anything. Period. If a parent is asked to buy something, they have the right to ask that it be granted to their child at no cost. Understand that schools are fraught with low budgets. Providing items or funds to a teacher or school is only acceptable if the parent chooses to do so. There should never be a grade attached to a child's ability to bring in a fee or supply.
  - **The right of immigrant children to a free education.** The US Supreme Court decided in 1982 that immigrant children have the same right to free Kindergarten to 12th grade public education as legalized United States children. There are few parameters. All children receive the same services. There is no need to present a visa, social security number, or other proof of citizenship to enroll a child.

- **The right to not be discriminated against.** Times are changing and this right is important to all students. No stereotype can inhibit a student from equal access to an education opportunity. For example, a student may not be excluded from an advanced placement class because they speak a different language or is pregnant. Or, a female has a right to take a construction class and a male has the right to take a sewing class. To go further, a gay child may invite a same-sex child to a school function.
- **Right to information.** A parent has the right to inspect their child's educational records per the *1974 Family Education Rights and Privacy Act (FERPA)*. The records are kept at the school or online. A parent may request corrections, additions or ask the records to be transferred to a non-public institution. *The 2015 Every Student Succeeds Act* further guarantees a parent-teacher conference, access to teachers, the right to ask for teacher qualifications, and more.
- **Rights of students with special needs or disabilities.** Parents have the legal right to request and receive an evaluation of their child's needs. These evaluations are at no cost to the parents. The schools and districts determine how the student's accommodation needs are met. A parent's signature is required as an acceptance of their student's Individual Education Plan (IEP) or Section 504.

❍ What is the difference between private and public services?

- Public schools receive public funding so they must follow what is required by the government overseers including federal, state and local entities. Private schools have a variety of funding sources from tuition, grants, and larger institutions related to religion or other entities. Private schools are free to offer alternative curriculums, varied schedules and education programs for specific groups, among other differences.

- Public schools accept all students within the school's zone or determined area of enrollment. Private schools have an admission process. This selection varies dependent on the school's direction and are not required to take all applicants.
- Public schools follow the government's requirement for teacher credentials and curriculum. Private schools may employee teachers without state teaching credentials. Curriculum for each course is set by the private school.
- Students with special needs may be denied entrance to a private school due to their inability to meet the student's Individual Education Plan (IEP) due to cost. Public schools are provided designated funding and require teacher training for serving the specific needs of students.
- Which school is best for the gifted student? Research beyond the parent grape vine is essential in gathering the facts to make an informed decision on school choice. A visit to the school and a meeting with the school leader and a teacher reveals the school's culture and priorities. Ask specific questions and visit a class in session. This is a highly personal family decision based on the student's interests and needs, family finances, and societal variables.

❍ Gather the troops – align with other parents

- Parent groups or simple friendships with parents of other students in the same school are important parts of raising a well-rounded child. These relationships provide a sense since of normalcy for the concerned parent. Conversations with parents of older students help new parents in a school navigate the complicated systems.
- One of the most rewarding adult relationships is the bonding between parents of children who are best friends.

This situation creates a "village" to raise the children in a protective circle of responsibility for each other's child.

- One parent is important. A group of parents is powerful. Parents have the ability to move a school or district to implement important initiatives or make changes.

❍ How does a parent navigate the school system?

- Start with the school leader. They can give a parent the policies and procedures in the larger school system. Their information of why the policies are in place is a great place to start an initiative to change the policy. The school staff has knowledge of who in the district has the ability to approve a change. The school leader frequently has less power to make change than a well informed and motivated group of parents.
- Confirm that all relevant information is based on fact. Gather documents to support the cause. Meet with the person who can change the policy, not the person who is charged with meeting with people who want to change the policy.
- Make the case for change. Accept the outcome or ask for the next step in changing the policy. This next step could be the school board or the state school board.

Reading Discussion Activities

1. What actions can a school team take to make their school more accommodating, friendly and informed for the parents of high achieving student.
2. Describe the school's culture in detail. How are the priorities of the school manifested in the physical school? What are the signs of the culture described?
3. Add your own "best practice for advocating for a student in school".

CHAPTER 21

The Act of Parenting in and out of School Through the Lens of a School Leader

The relationship between a school leader and their student's parents is enriching and rewarding. Each parent wants the best education for their child. Each administrator works diligently to meet the academic and social needs of all students in the school. This is a partnership. The parent has experience with a small number of children. The school administrator may have experienced thousands of students and as many parents in their career. This does not preclude a unique situation occurring each school year.

A school leader is called to be student-centered while providing supports to parents. The list below includes a few highlights drawn from actual experiences. Some may be controversial, but many situations repeat year after year with different students and different parents.

Take a Nugget or Two with the Understanding that each Child and Situation are Unique

Asynchronous development (different talents at different times)

- Child development is just that: development. Changes occur on a constant basis. Stay alert, aware and supportive of these changes as they occur.

- Comparing a child's past success when they fail is not endorsed. They are experiencing physical, mental and emotional changes at all times.
- Their past talents grow into different talents. Celebrate who they are in the present time.

Monitor and supplement the school's curriculum: know what the child is learning.

- Enjoy conversations with the child about the curricular content. It is widely known that the world is political. These conversations with the family teach the child how to evaluate information from a different perspective.
- Parents have the power to provide a balance of information.
- Celebrate the family's heritage through historically and culturally augmenting curriculum.

"I really don't want to be in the smart kid classes." Walk through the reasons for this statement with the child.

- Why do they feel this way? Is there bullying present? There may be an "alpha" student who is pressuring other students to stay below them on the class's "smart" scale. Take action if this is the reason. Bullying is not tolerated in schools. Seek administrative support.
- If the student simply does not want attention, speak to the teacher about keeping successes mum.

Watch for telling behaviors and check up on what they tell you.

- Regardless of age, most students are two to three steps ahead of their parents.
- *Respect* the information given by the child but *inspect* the information. Such inspection can occur with little effort. The parent is aware of the child's resources.
- The consequences for untruthfulness or misbehavior should be known prior to the occurrence. This method makes it

obvious that the child chooses to have the consequences when they choose to misbehave. Always follow through on the established consequences.

- Here are common buzzwords of minor offenses: "everyone hates that teacher, everyone failed that test, I asked her, and she didn't have time for me, everyone is going to be there, so I have to go, she loses everyone's homework, so nobody turns in homework…"

Parents only know what the student wants them to know.

- Students may keep information from parents because they want to have it to themselves. This is not a slight on the parent. It is a choice made to exercise independence.
- It is critical for parents to know negative or harmful information. The parental instincts through keen observation will recognize when this information needs to be nurtured out of the child.
- It is not unusual for the school staff to have information that the parent does not. This is a tightrope. Each situation is considered independently with regard to the student's safety and parental responsibilities.

Students know the parent's buttons.

- Be aware of the child's knowledge of what makes their parents react. If a parent is feeling guilty about a divorce, move, past drug use, etc. the child may use this emotion to get what they want. Not reacting emotionally is the parent's best weapon to combat this maneuvering.
- Manipulating a parent's weaknesses to gain favor is normal. However, be aware and call out the child when this occurs.

Do not overreact or over punish

- An effective practice is to have the consequences to a behavior already in place prior to the offense. The child is choosing to risk the consequence by misbehaving.

- Punishing for poor grades is rarely successful. Taking away prized possessions such as cell phones or gaming devices rarely incentivizes learning. Students will do what they want to do and how they want to do it. A parent's anger may be the reaction they wanted.
- Consider providing incentives or rewards for good grades instead of punishments. Include the family on these incentives such as an outing or new TV, etc. Sometimes it takes a tribe to put the pressure on the child to let go of bad habits.

Don't give too many choices but give choices.

- The elementary student is allowed to choose between the blue or green socks. Do not tell them to wear the blue socks. This is simple, but important to a maturing child.
- When they enter adolescence, children demand and need to make their own choices. Give them a limited (two or three) options instead of telling them what to do.
- As teens, they will make choices without the parent's knowledge. They know the choice the parent wants them to select. They may choose to not follow what their parents want, simply to display their personal control. Give them control of everything safely possible in their world. Then…monitor constantly and closely. Give choices for important matters which the parent wants to control. (You may attend Harvard or Princeton, but not Berkley.)

Self-sabotage is real and occurs in every school during every school year.

- The student is in control of their choice to excel in school. They will use this control to meet their parent's expectations or not meet their parent's expectations.
- Caution: Students will take actions to hurt themselves as a means of control. Common actions are failing classes, stopping eating, partaking in illegal drugs, disappearing, dating controversial people, attempting suicide, running away, etc.

- Wise parents will know when to give in. Do not wait until the child harms themselves.

Parenting a unique child.

- Friends are a great confidence builder for children who are different from their peers. Find them. Search for like interests. Many times, this will be intellectual pursuits such as chess, robotics, scouting, engineering clubs, etc.
- Seek out parents with similar students. These adult relationships create a foundation of support for the entire household. The school staff has resources to find family matches.

Appropriate role models cannot be over emphasized.

- It is a child's natural instinct to follow a mentor. Consider this human "imprinting." A parent has the power to select these models. Place these mentors in the child's path.
- Ideas for possible mentors outside of the parents: grandparents, older siblings, older students, neighbors, church leaders, businesspeople, teachers, coaches, administration, student's choice: listen to who they admire.

Peer environments with fellow gifted students.

- Creating situations for the student to socialize with similar peers builds confidence and a sense of belonging which has the potential to last a lifetime.
- Isolation is not an option for a maturing child. Parent intervention is critical. Loneliness is a caustic situation which only gets worse with depression, anxiety and behavior issues.
- Create "play dates" for all ages of students. This is easier with younger students. But also possible for older students: Drop offs for theme parks, pizza parties at home, after school "clubs" at home on specific days of the week (may include homework and snacks), Saturday outings in the community, etc. Communicate with several parents to share the activity schedule and transportation.

Disabilities or mental health problems

- Parents are encouraged to communicate with the school's leader or counselor regarding their student's unique needs.
- It is not good practice to "just see what happens" in the next school year. Bring the school staff into the relationship with the student. These staff members are fellow student advocates. The start of a new school year is not the time to stop medications or experiment with the child's ability to manage their disability.
- Disabilities are vast and frequently not physically apparent. Alert the school student advocates if the child has attention deficit syndrome, depression, paranoia, anxiety or physical conditions such as a heart condition, seizures, hormone imbalances, etc.

The first failing grade…it is going to happen.

- Stay silent and watch the child's reaction.
- The student may be harder on themselves than the parent. Give them time to soak in the parent's response to the grade. Then, listen to their explanation.
- There may be a need to re-order priorities. Let the student determine how to solve the problem.
- Perfection has the power to be destructively negative or motivationally positive. The parent wants balance.
- Stay in communication with the teacher to glean the facts. Do not fall for the buzz word excuses: everyone failed this assignment, we had a substitute, she graded it wrong, etc.

Homework—to help or not to help?

- Know what is assigned for homework. Go through the list each afternoon or evening. Allow the student to decide the timeframe of each assignment. Always start with the subject that is disliked. This is important. They will not try as hard on the last homework subject. The subject they dislike is probably the one that needs the most mental energy. This works for all ages – even adults.

- Know how the student learns. Repetition may not work. But analysis and conversation may be what places the information into long term memory.
- If the parent is talking more than the student. That is not helping. That is doing.
- Have the student teach the parent the subject. This may occur after the student finishes their homework and the parent is checking that all is completed.

Organizational skills will take a child a long way and produce higher functioning adults.

- The student's planner is monitored by the parent. This works for any age.
- The supplies are not an issue because the parent provides everything needed on time and in abundance. This is one stressor the parent can take off the student's plate.
- Time schedules are paramount for success. Create a schedule each school year. It is adaptable based on new information (added afterschool activity, poor grades, etc.) only after the parent and student agree.

What can parents do to nurture gifted students into adulthood?

- Ask any teacher this question and they will answer "make students responsible for their own behavior."
- Parents have the power to create confident adults by holding students accountable for their choices while positively nurturing them as they travel the bumpy road through their childhood.
- Constantly model respect for authority. Teach students how and when to self-advocate with respect. Do not "have the

school" for dinner. Negative talk in the home about any aspect of the school will translate into the child's behavior in school. This is a proven fact.

- Support the adult advocates around the student by encouraging the child to speak with them when needed.

Elementary students should stay with their pack

- The gifted elementary student is an emotional being wanting to fit in with the pack.
- Select the pack and keep the members and their parents close.
- Neighborhood kids or friends outside of school may not be in the desired pack. These friends are situational and may not align with the child's personality or giftedness.
- Yes, the child needs to have a well-rounded group of friends. But, navigate these differences carefully. These young years can be the last time a parent has the power to select their child's influencing friends.

Six going on sixteen and beyond

- The child is smarter than the adults in their world. Congratulations, your child is smarter than you. Obviously, the cognitive abilities are not matching the physical or physiological maturity of the child.
- The parent's role is to help the child manage these differences. A well-informed parent will seek out mentors, similar parents and research to foster their child's growth.
- Be acutely aware that the child can out-think the parent with their rationale or ability to predict a parent's reaction.
- Listen to the child's concerns and worries often. They will change with each day or situation. This exercise provides the parent with the "play book" on helping their child adjust to highly functioning in a lower functioning world.

Middle school kids are just weird

- This is not the same child who was in elementary school a few months ago. There is a collision of physical, emotional, social and physiological elements occurring at the speed of light each day in an adolescent's life.
- The gifted student is no exception to the trials faced during the maturing process in middle school. Embrace this process with cautious support and constant supervision.
- Bond with other middle school parents. Volunteer at school. This is a good activity for all middle school parents because this is an opportunity to see that their child is not so weird after all.
- This is the time to set strict schedules, avoid overreacting to anything (they will top your over reaction), stay consistent with all things, be available for conversations, be present in the home, be OK not getting the last word in during an argument and give choices for all aspects in the home. This is not the time to divorce, move, adopt a child or otherwise upset the child's world.
- Listen to the middle school teachers and school leaders. They have chosen to work with this age group and have enjoyed thousands of experiences. Ask direct questions and learn from their experiences.
- One way to get an adolescent's attention when their world is crashing down on them and they are in a dark spiral of emotion is to let them drive your car in a very large empty parking lot. This will work every time. Its free, safe, adultlike and builds trust.

I am so different from everyone in school. Will you home school me?

- This request from any age of student is situational. The parent needs to research the genesis of the question. Ask the student what occurred to make them feel different. Ensure that the child is placed in the correct class. Are they in a gifted class or does the school have gifted pull-out opportunities? Ask about the other students in the class. Listen for any signs of bullying. Follow up with the school leaders with concerns.

- The home school request is often the result of the child speaking with a homeschooled student. This situation may be attractive: staying home all day, eating lunch with mom, playing outside every day, working on a computer all day, going on fieldtrips every day, etc. An explanation of what occurs during home schooling may provide a reality check for the child.

Parent advocacy and support for schools & vice versa

- Parents are encouraged to actively participate in the school environment. The activities may not be with the students. Volunteering to be on the parent boards or school improvement counsels provides a knowledge of the school's operation and insight on personnel and budgets.

- Supporting the initiatives of the school leaders is important. Get to know the school leader and ask about their goals for the school. Volunteer to be a supportive spokesperson for other parents or the school district.

Build community parent groups

- Each school has a parent group which is on a spectrum of function. Some groups need strong leaders to get them started and create a reason for existing. Other groups have strong leaders and set agendas for their annual activities. Each of these types of groups need volunteers who are passionate about creating great experiences for children.

- Parent groups are attended by the school leaders. This is an opportunity to ask questions and seek answers to school or personal issues. The parent has the school leader at their disposal without a telephone call or office visit. Additionally, school leaders are more likely to be relaxed and flexible in these parent group settings. This is the time to ask for a favor or spill the beans on important school-related information.

- Build parent groups that orchestrate ideas on school improvement.

Have an open dialogue with the principal. Hold your administration accountable.

- The school leader's secretary or "gate keeper" should know the parent as a kind and generous person who makes them feel valued. This is important.
- Speak praises to the school leaders. These short, nice hallway or car pick-up line conversations are priceless to overworked and tired administrators.
- When a problem arises, enter the meeting, conference, etc. with at least three viable solutions.
- Show respect for the student and expect respect from the student at all times in the presence of school staff.

Create quality gifted-centered community programs:

- Develop and market activities for advanced learners to develop their skills and creativity.
- Find facilitators from industries other than schools to lead programs for the high-ability students.
- Get involved with the local, state or national gifted organization. The meetings are attended by gifted advocates. Parents are encouraged to join the networking voices who advocate for gifted education.

Reading Discussion Activities

1. Select one of the "nuggets" in the chapter. Write or discuss your experience, or lack of experience with the situation. Write or discuss your reflection on how to proceed with a gifted advocate mindset.
2. Write 2 – 3 additional "nuggets" from your experiences which reflect a gifted parent advocate mindset.
3. As a school leader or as a parent of a gifted student, what advice would you give a new family of a gifted student in your school.

Closing

All parents want what is best for their children. The interpretation of "best" is a moving target through the school years. The child changes as much as the systems that are called to prepare students for the adult world as a functional wage-earning civilian. There is no child advocate with more passion than their parent. Successful school leaders manage their expectations and communications with this realization. They are responsible for the safety and education of a student. School leaders are equally responsible for serving the parents of each student.

Parents who acknowledge their need for information and direction from a school system are most successful when they prepare themselves to listen to viable solutions and opinions. As expressed above, approach the information-gathering task well-informed and pleasantly assertive. The school environment should be set up to serve the parent's needs.

This book is a resource that provides a parent with insider knowledge of how a school has the ability to serve the advanced learner. The knowledge and tactics gained from these pages provides the parent with tools to address the issues with the school staff. Use this information in the quest to find solutions for the student.

Parenting high level learners demands consistently stretching a child from a status quo toward high expectations. Parents have the ability to be a model of the good stewardship of intelligence. Failures, decisions, successes, compassion, empathy, organization, communication and more, need to be modeled by all adults in a child's life. The gifted student is constantly making choices. This positive modeling and using the information in this section is essential to healthy social and emotional growth.

As a child passes through the lives of their parents, lessons are learned. What are the lessons an experienced parent can share with others starting their journey? Share these valuable experiences often. Watch and assess how this knowledge can help other parents. Gather the parents of gifted students. As expressed on these pages, these communities are invaluable.

Where to go for help? Reading this resource is a start in gathering the knowledge needed to assist the gifted learner. Follow up with school leaders, school counselors, teachers and fellow parents. They are waiting in a circle of support for students. Reach out early and often.

Final Thoughts

A school leader has the ultimate responsibility of preparing all the students in their school to thrive in the world following graduation. There is an expectation they have the knowledge of how to serve each level of learner and especially, their diverse students. Does every school leader meet this expectation? Absolutely not. It takes study, experimentation, research, mentoring and the courage to implement a student-centered initiative. It takes courage to follow a path that is different from one's predecessors.

Conformity is the jailer of freedom and the enemy of growth.

John F. Kennedy

The leadership style of a school leader drives their desire and ability to stretch the learning of each student. Are they a visionary or a task-oriented leader? It is easy to notice a better learning environment is needed. It is the next step toward action that proves one is a powerful student-centered leader. The students reveal their needs. Use this book as a resource to develop an educated lens of what is needed in the school's gifted education. Watch and act.

The parents of gifted children look to their child's school for answers on how to serve their children. Their partnership is a pivotal component to graduating a student who possesses the tools to embrace and adapt their giftedness to life's future challenges.

The quality of a student's future can be changed by the tweaks the school leader makes in their school. These pages serve as a resource of information designed to elevate the learning environment for all children. The advanced learner is the focus, yet the principles are easily adapted to all levels of learners. Start with a few small changes or delve in and create a wave of action toward serving gifted and other diverse learners in a successful student-centered school.

The school leader has the power. Use it for a better and greater school improvement. Start the exploration with an evaluation of what a well-prepared gifted adult needs to possess as they leave secondary education. Then, take the steps to make it happen. Do not stop until the least learner is at the top of their learning capacity scale. The resources are waiting to be mined.

These bright students have the capacity to solve the world's most complicated problems. The school leader gives them the tools to get started on their quest to positively affect all of society. Their incredible minds are fertile soil waiting for their advocates to plant the seeds of confidence, optimism, strength and abilities early and often. Simply prepare the soil, these high-level learners will guarantee the growth. Give them the nurturing tools and the space to learn without limitation. Remove the weeds, or barriers, that choke out their progress.

The nation's most valuable natural resource, the gifted child, is waiting for the school leader's intervention and protection. If leaders implement these strategies in every school the results will be endless. Watch how diseases are cured, governments are more productive, the economy grows, and the environment is cleaned. Start with this and other resources on serving the gifted student through the encouragement of the building of a gifted community of support.

Appendices

The 4 Appendices are included here.

They are attachments due to their unique formatting.

1. Appendix A: Registration Fair Set up and Agenda
2. Appendix B.1: Individualized Student Registration Sheet: 9th Grade Core (front)
3. Appendix B.2: Individualized Student Registration Sheet: 10th Grade Electives (back)
4. Appendix C: Teacher Preference Survey

Appendix A: Registration Fair Set up and Agenda

APPENDIX A

Lead Smart High School
Staff Information for the Registration Fair Set up and Agenda

LeadSmart
education + innovation

January 15th, 8am – 7pm

Calendar of Implementation

October:
- √ Preparation for Registration Fair, delegation of duties
- √ Student Registration course options finalized
- √ 1st week: Teacher Preference Survey results in spreadsheet
- √ Invitations to community members who participate (business partners, coaches, club sponsors, etc.)
- √ Organize and assign teacher and parent volunteers

November:
- √ Preparation for Registration Fair
- √ Confirm facilities requirements and community participants
- √ Order print materials
- √ Prepare digital movie for processes and course information

December: *(first week)*
- √ Media blitz notifications of upcoming registration process
- √ All Forms and Registration options finalized
- √ Teachers, clubs, athletics confirm the contents and staffing of their table set ups.

January:
- √ *(week after Winter Break)* Online Pre-Registration Open: Information Forms, course selections vary
- √ Personalized Student Registration Forms printed from online information for distribution at fair.
- √ Preparation for Registration Fair.
- √ Registration Fair: 3rd week of January
- √ Last week of January: collect registration data, answer online questions on registration page.

Staff Responsibilities
- √ *Principal:* Delegation and follow up,
- √ *Assistant Principals/Deans:*
  - o 1/Curriculum: online registration forms, data spreadsheets
  - o 2/Counselors: Core and Elective set ups, Auditorium set up, schedule
  - o 3/Business Partnership Contact and set up, facility and custodial set up
- √ *Counselors:* prepare hard copy registration forms, all other forms, present in auditorium with a teacher, organize teachers and support staff at their tables.
- √ *Media Specialist*: organize helpers to: confirm and collect all forms, download texts for classes on student devices (after registration complete for core, may not apply to electives)
- √ *Special Education Supervisor:* at tables, organized teachers to help by specialty
- √ *Teachers:* designated to areas by administration
- √ *Athletic Director:* organizes gym for athletics and clubs, schedules staff and students to man tables, all are accountable for their own display.
- √ *IT Specialist:* Check out rental devices, confirm and assist with internet in the home, etc. Oversees team who assists parents with the completion of all online forms in various languages during registration.

Appendix B.1: Individualized Student Registration Sheet: 9th Grade Core (front)

Lead Smart HS Registration (IB High School) — **2020-2021 Course Registration** — **9th Grade**

Student Name: __John Dillinger____________________
Student ID Number __8675301____________________
Student Telephone # __800-123-4567____(cell)______________
Student Email __J.dillinger@edu.xxx__________________
Student Home Language: ______________________________
School Counselor Notes:

Parent/Guardian Name __Ms. Janice Dillinger______________
Parent/Guardian Telephone # __800-765-4321__________________
Parent Email __janice.dillinger@edu.xxx___________
Student Exceptionalities: ______________________________
Dates for Review Exceptionality: ______________________________
Other Information

*Place an **X** is next to your required course for each subject area. Elective courses are on the 2nd page. Refer to the LSHS Curriculum Guide for course description located at www.LSHS@edu.xxx. Complete all forms (include your parents) on line prior to the Registration Fair.*

		Grade 9	Grade 10	Grade 11	Grade 12
Studies in Language & Literature	X	*Pre-IB English 1*	*Pre-IB English 2*	**AP English Composition**	**IB English 4** **AP English Literature**
Individual & Societies	X	*Government (first semester)*	Advanced Placement United States History	**IB Contemporary History 1**	**IB Contemporary History 2**
	X	*Economics (second semester)*			
Mathematics		*Algebra 2 Honors* (prerequisite Geometry)	**IB Pre-Calculus** (prereq B or higher in Alg 2)	**Advanced Placement Calculus AB/IB Math SL**	**Advanced Placement Calculus BC**
	X	*Geometry Honors*	*Algebra 2 Honors*	**IB Pre-Calculus**	**Advanced Placement Calculus AB/IB Math SL**
				IB Stats/Differential Cal SL	**Advanced Placement Calculus**
				IB Math Studies	**IB Stats/Differential Cal SL**
Sciences	X	*Pre-IB Biology*		**Advanced Placement Biology**	**IB Biology 3 HL**
	X	**Advanced Placement Environmental Science**	*Pre-IB Chemistry*	**Advanced Placement Chemistry**	**IB Chemistry 3 HL**
			Pre-IB Physics	**Advanced Placement Physics 1: Algebra-Based**	**IB Physics 3 HL/AP Physics 2: Algebra-Based**
Language Acquisition		*Pre-IB French 1*	*Pre-IB French 2/3*	**IB French 4**	**Advanced Placement French/IB French 5**
		Pre-IB German 1	*Pre-IB German 2/3*	**IB German 4**	**Advanced Placement German/IB German 5**
		Pre-IB Spanish 2	*Pre-IB Spanish 3*	**Advanced Placement Spanish**	**IB Spanish 5**
Sixth Subject/ Academy Elective		Select Elective	Select Elective	Select Elective	Select Elective
		Pre-IB Art 1	*Pre-IB Art 2*	**IB Art B1 SL**	**IB Art B2 SL**
		Pre-IB Music 1 Band	*Pre-IB Music 2* – Band	**IB Music 1** – Band	**IB Art B3 HL**
		Pre-IB Music1 – Chorus	*Pre-IB Music 2* – Chorus	**IB Music 1** – Chorus	**IB Music 2 SL** – Band
		Pre-IB Music Orchestra	*Pre-IB Music 2/* Orchestra	**IB Music 1** – Orchestra	**Music 2 SL** – Chorus
				IB Business & Mgmt 2 SL	**IB Music 2 SL** – Orchestra
				IB Psychology 2 SL	**IB Music 3 HL**
IB Requirement				**Theory of Knowledge** (Second Semester)	**Theory of Knowledge** (First Semester)

APPENDIX B.1

Date Revised:

Appendix B.2: Individualized Student Registration Sheet: 10th Grade Electives (back)

APPENDIX B.2

10th GRADE - SOPHOMORE ELECTIVES

Number 1 through 10 in order of preference, with '1' being your top choice.

Academy of Culinary & Agrisciences

CULINARY SCIENCE ACADEMY

___ Culinary Arts 1
___ Culinary Arts 2

AGRISCIENCE ACADEMY

___ Agri-Science Foundations
___ Intro. to Horticulture Sci 2
___ Agri.Tech 1
___ Vet. & Animal Science 2

Academy of Engineering and Construction

CONSTRUCTION ACADEMY

___ Cabinetmaking 1
___ Cabinetmaking 2

ENGINEERING ACADEMY

___ Applied Engineering Tech 1
___ Applied Engineering Tech 2

Academy of Arts

PERFORMING ART ACADEMY

___ Band 1
___ Intermediate Band 2
___ Percussion 1
___ Percussion 2
___ ***Jazz must also take Band***
___ Jazz Ensemble 1
___ Jazz Ensemble 2
___ Instrum Tech/Percussion 1
___ Instrum Tech/Percussion 2
___ Chorus1 (Women's Choir)
___ Chorus 2
___ Vocal Ensemble 1
___ Vocal Ensemble 2
___ Theater 1
___ Theater 2
___ Orchestra 1
___ Orchestra 2

VISUAL ARTS ACADEMY

___ 2-D Studio Art 1
___ 2-D Studio Art 2
___ Drawing 1
___ Drawing 2
___ 3-D Studio Art 1
___ 3-D Studio Art 2
___ Creative Photography
___ Creative Photography 2
___ AP Art History

Law Academy & Medical Academy

LEGAL STUDIES ACADEMY

___ Legal Office Tech 1
(prerequisite Legal Aspects of Bus.)
___ Legal Office Tech 2

MEDICAL ACADEMY

___ Health Science 1
___ Health Science 2
___ Emergency Medical Responder
___ EKG Directed Study/Aide

Academy of Design

DIGITAL PRODUCTIONS

___ TV Productions 1
___ TV Productions 2

DIGITAL DESIGN

___ Digital Design 2 Honors
___ Digital Design 3 Honors

Sports Academy

SPORTS ACADEMY

All P.E. classes are semester classes and paired for the school year as follows:

___ Personal Fitness 1st Sem.
___ Sports Officiating 2nd Sem

___ Basketball 1st Sem.
___ Softball 2nd Sem.

___ Beg. Weight Train 1st Sem
___ Int. Weight Train 2nd Sem

___ Adv. Weight Train 1st Sem
___ Power Weight Train 2nd Sem

___ Beg. Aerobics 1st Sem.
___ Beg. Volleyball 2nd Sem.
___ Inter. Volleyball 1st Sem.
___ Adv. Volleyball 2nd Sem.

Registration Fair
January 13th

Academic Electives

ENGLISH ELECTIVES

___ Creative Write 1/Creative Write 2
___ Journalism

SCIENCE ELECTIVES

___ Anatomy & Physiology Honors
___ Forensic Science (elective credit)
___ Astronomy (elective credit)
___ AP Environmental Science

SOCIAL STUDIES ELECTIVES

___ Psychology / Sociology
___ Philosophy Honors / Law Studies
___ AP Human Geography
___ AP European History
___ AP Psychology
___ AP Art History

WORLD LANGUAGES

___ Spanish 1
___ Spanish 2
___ Spanish 2 Honors
___ Spanish 3 Honors
___ French 1
___ French 2
___ French 2 Honors
___ German 1
___ German 2 Honors

(AP = Advanced Placement)

Go to: LSHS@edu.xxx
Complete as much information as possible online prior to the Registration Fair.

Your *Personalized Registration Sheet* will be printed and provided for you when you arrivel at the fair.

Visit Elective and Club Tables!
Bring your Parents.

Student Email: ______________________

Parent Contact Information: ______________________

Parent Email: ______________________

Date: ______________________

Rev: Date

Appendix C: Teacher Preference Survey

APPENDIX C

Lead Smart Elementary School

Teacher Preference Survey

Return to Dr. Small's office by: October 14th

LeadSmart
education + innovation

Thank you for completing this confidential LSES ***Teacher Preference Survey***.

This information is important in our planning for the next school year. Please provide your "wish list" for your teaching position. As always, I am always available to discuss your preferences.
Additional information will be used to update our records.

Full Name	
Best Contact Number	
Personal Email	
Mailing Address	
Additional Important Information	
State Certification(s)	
Additional Certifications or Endorsements & those in progress*	
Current Teaching Assignment (subject & grade level)	
First Preferred Subject	
Second Preferred Subject	
Third Preferred Subject	
First Preferred Grade Level	
Second Preferred Grade Level	
Third Preferred Grade Level	
Classroom location Preference, indicate why?	
Planning Period preference	
Confidential Comments:	

*National Board Certified, Endorsements: English Language Learners, Gifted, Exceptional Education, etc.

Teacher Preference Survey *Date Revised:*

Notes

PART ONE

Chapter 1

1 Ed Week (2009), https://www.edweek.org/media/2019/11/25/gt%20survey%20report-final%2011.25.19.pdf.

2 NAGC.org, National Association of Gifted Children. How many gifted children are in the US? https://www.nagc.org/resources-publications/resources/frequently-asked-questions-about-gifted-education.

3 OCR.ed.gov, Office of Civil Rights, https://nces.ed.gov/programs/digest/d17/tables/dt17_204.90.asp.

4 Neuschel, Robert P. (2005) The Servant Leader, unleashing the power of your people. Kellogg School of Management, Northwestern University Press.

5 CDE, 2020, (Colorado Department of Education) https://www.cde.state.co.us/gt.

Chapter 2

1 NAGC.org, Definition of Gifted, https://www.nagc.org/sites/default/files/administrators/Rationale%20for%20Gifted%20Ed.pdf.

2 Columbus Group, (1991). https://educationaladvancement.org/blog-5-definitions-of-giftedness/.

3 NAGC.org, Jacob Javits, https://www.nagc.org/resources-publications/resources-university-professionals/jacob-javits-gifted-talented-students.

4 US Department of Education, https://www2.ed.gov/policy/elsec/leg/esea02/pg107.html.

5 US Education Commission, https://www.ecs.org/?s=gifted+definition.

6 Clark, B. (2008). *Growing up gifted* (7th ed.) Upper Saddle River, NJ: Pearson Prentice Hall.

7 NAGC, Gifted Child Quarterly, Fall, 2009, https://www.nagc.org/myths-about-gifted-students.

8 NAGC.org, National Association of Gifted Children. Characteristics of gifted children. https://www.nagc.org/resources-publications/resources/my-child-gifted/common-characteristics-gifted-individuals/traits. Clark, B. (2008). *Growing up gifted* (7th ed.) Upper Saddle River, NJ: Pearson Prentice Hall.

9 Clance, P.R. & Imes, S. (1978). The impostor phenomenon in high achieving women: Dynamics and therapeutic intervention. *Psychotherapy: Theory, Research and Practice*, 15, 241–247.

10 Silverman, L.K., What We Have Learned About Gifted Children, Gifted Development Center, embracing giftedness. https://web.archive.org/web/20140216195224/http://www.gifteddevelopment.com:80/What_is_Gifted/learned.htm. Retrieved October 2020.

11 Alias A, Rahman S, Majid RA, Yassin SFM. Dabrowski's Overexcitabilities Profile among Gifted Students. *Asian Social Science*. 2013;9(16). doi:10.5539/ass. v9n16p120.

12 The Anxiety-Free Child Program, (2013). Is Your Child Anxious Because They're Gifted? advanced strategies for overcoming your child's anxiety. https://anxietyfreechild.com/gifted-children/.

13 Post, G., (2013). Gifted Challenges, a life lesson for gifted children: failure. Simple Theme. https://giftedchallenges.blogspot.com/2013/08/a-life-lesson-for-gifted-children.html.

14 Berlin, J.E., (2009) It's All a Matter of Perspective: Student Perceptions on the Impact of Being Labeled Gifted and Talented, *Roeper Review*, 31(4): 217-223. https://www.researchgate.net/publication/232971537_It%27s_All_a_Matter_of_Perspective_Student_Perceptions_on_the_Impact_of_Being_Labeled_Gifted_and_Talented.

15 CC-BY-SA, Byrdseed, LLC. https://www.byrdseed.com/10-facts-about-social-emotional-needs-of-the-gifted/.

16 Naglieri, J., Brulles, D., Lansdowne, K., (2008). *Helping All Gifted Children Learn, A Teacher's Guide to Using the NNAT2.* Pearson Education, Inc.

Chapter 3

1 Findlaw, https://education.findlaw.com/education-options/compulsory-education-laws-background.html.

2 Colangelo, N., Assouline, S., Gross, M. (2004). A nation deceived: how schools hold back America's brightest students. Iowa City, Iowa: The Connie Belin & Jacqueline N. Blank International Center for Gifted Education and Talent Development, University of Iowa.

3. Colangelo, N., Assouline, S., Gross, M. (2004). A nation deceived: how schools hold back America's brightest students. Iowa City, Iowa: The Connie Belin & Jacqueline N. Blank International Center for Gifted Education and Talent Development, University of Iowa.

4 Assouline, S. G., Colangelo, N., Gross, M. U. M., Templeton Foundation., Connie Belin & Jacqueline N. Blank International Center for Gifted Education and Talent Development., & National Association for Gifted Children (U.S.). (2015). *A Nation Empowered: Evidence Trumps the Excuses Holding Back America's Brightest Students.* Iowa City, Iowa: Connie Belin & Jacqueline N. Blank International Center for Gifted Education and Talent Development, University of Iowa.

5 Stephens K.R. (2018) Applicable Federal and State Policy, Law, and Legal Considerations in Gifted Education. In: Pfeiffer S. (eds) Handbook of Giftedness in Children. Springer, Cham. https://doi.org/10.1007/978-3-319-77004-8_11.

6 NDEA: Pub. L. No. 85-864, 72 Stat. 1580.

7 ESEA: Pub. L. No. 89-10, 79 Stat. 27 (codified as amended in scattered sections of 20 U.S.C.

8 Stephens K.R. (2018) Applicable Federal and State Policy, Law, and Legal Considerations in Gifted Education. In: Pfeiffer S. (eds) Handbook of Giftedness in Children. Springer, Cham. https://doi.org/10.1007/978-3-319-77004-8_11.

9 MR1972: Education Amendments of 1974, Pub. L. No. 93-380, § 404(a), 88 Stat. 484, 547 (section repealed in 1979).

10 GTCEA: Pub. L. No. 95-561, §§ 901–08, 92 Stat. 2143, 2292–96 (amending ESEA as part of the Education Amendments of 1978) (repealed 1982).

11 Stephens K.R. (2018) Applicable Federal and State Policy, Law, and Legal Considerations in Gifted Education. In: Pfeiffer S. (eds) Handbook of Giftedness in Children. Springer, Cham. https://doi.org/10.1007/978-3-319-77004-8_11.

12 JGTSEA: Pub. L. No. 100-297, §§ 4101–08, 102 Stat. 130, 237–40 (codified as amended at 20 U.S.C. §§ 7253–7253e (2006)) (amending ESEA as part of the Augustus F. Hawkins-Robert T. Stafford Elementary and Secondary School Improvement Amendments of 1988).

13 NCLB: Pub. L. No. 107-110, 115 Stat. 1425 (codified as amended in scattered sections of 20 U.S.C.) (amending ESEA).

14 IDEA: Most recently passed as Individuals with Disabilities Education Improvement Act of 2004, Pub. L. No. 108-446, 118 Stat. 2647.

15 Stephens K.R. (2018) Applicable Federal and State Policy, Law, and Legal Considerations in Gifted Education. In: Pfeiffer S. (eds) Handbook of Giftedness in Children. Springer, Cham. https://doi.org/10.1007/978-3-319-77004-8_11.

16 Stephens K.R. (2018) Applicable Federal and State Policy, Law, and Legal Considerations in Gifted Education. In: Pfeiffer S. (eds) Handbook of Giftedness in Children. Springer, Cham. https://doi.org/10.1007/978-3-319-77004-8_11.

17 Stephens K.R. (2018) Applicable Federal and State Policy, Law, and Legal Considerations in Gifted Education. In: Pfeiffer S. (eds) Handbook of Giftedness in Children. Springer, Cham. https://doi.org/10.1007/978-3-319-77004-8_11.

18 Davidson Institute for Talent Development, https://www.davidsongifted.org/search-database/entrytype/3.

PART TWO

Chapter 6

1 Belin-Blank, 2020, Acceleration Institute at the Belin-Blank Center, College of Education, University of Iowa, http://www.accelerationinstitute.org/Resources/QA/.

2 Holloway, J., (2003) Research Link/Grouping Gifted Student, *Education Leadership*, October 2003, V61, 2, pp 89-91.

3 Naglieri, J., Brulles, D., Lansdowne, K., (2008). *Helping All Gifted Children Learn, A Teacher's Guide to Using the NNAT2.* Pearson Education, Inc.

Chapter 7

1 Forgotten Middle Summary, (2020), https://www.act.org/content/act/en/research/pdfs/the-forgotten-middleresearchstudy.html.

2 Belin-Blank Center, (2020) Acceleration Institute at the Belin-Blank Center, 20 Types of Acceleration, http://www.accelerationinstitute.org/Acceleration_Explained/acceleration_types.aspx.

3 McFarland, C., & Buehler, R. (1995). Collective self-esteem as a moderator of the frog-pond effect in reactions to performance feedback. *Journal of Personality and Social Psychology, 68*, 1055-1070.

4 Frog Pond Theory Resource: NOBA is the Diener Education Fund, a non-profit organization. https://nobaproject.com/modules/social-comparison, visualization of the theory: https://www.youtube.com/watch?v=1p3X-iFCWqA.

5 Naglieri, J., Brulles, D., Lansdowne, K., (2008). *Helping All Gifted Children Learn, A Teacher's Guide to Using the NNAT2.* Pearson Education, Inc.

6 Colangelo, N., Assouline, S., Gross, M. (2004). A nation deceived: how schools hold back America's brightest students. Iowa City, Iowa: The Connie Belin & Jacqueline N. Blank International Center for Gifted Education and Talent Development, University of Iowa.

7 Belin-Blank Acceleration Institute, (2020), Iowa Acceleration Scale, http://www.accelerationinstitute.org/Tools/IAS.aspx.

8 Strauss, V. (2019). What Exactly is an "underachiever," and Why are there so many of them in our schools? Citation from Saiying Steenbergen-Hu on gifted underachiever research, *Washington Post,* July 5, 2019. https://www.washingtonpost.com/education/2019/07/05/what-exactly-is-an-underachiever-why-are-there-so-many-them-our-schools/.

9 Belin-Blank Center Acceleration Institute, (2020), 20 Types of Acceleration, http://www.accelerationinstitute.org/Acceleration_Explained/acceleration_types.aspx.

Chapter 8

1 *Appendix B.*1: Individualized Student Registration Sheet: 9th Grade Core (front).

2 *Appendix B.2:* Individualized Student Registration Sheet: 10th Grade Electives (back)

3 *Appendix C:* Teacher Preference Survey

Chapter 9

1 Neila A. Connors Quote, Outstanding educator, author and speaker, learn more about Dr. Connors: https://www.educationspeakersgroup.com/n_connors.html

2 Farkas, S. & Duffet, A. (2008). Results from a national teacher survey. In Thomas B. Fordham Institute, High Achievement students in the era of NCLB (p.78). Washington, DC: Author. http://www.edexcellence.net/publications/high-achieving-studentts-in.html.

3 Naglieri, J., Brulles, D., Lansdowne, K., (2008). *Helping All Gifted Children Learn, A Teacher's Guide to Using the NNAT2.* Pearson Education, Inc.

4 Naglieri, J., Brulles, D., Lansdowne, K., (2008). *Helping All Gifted Children Learn, A Teacher's Guide to Using the NNAT2.* Pearson Education, Inc.

Chapter 12

1 CTSA, Career Technical Student Organization, https://www.aeseducation.com/blog/career-technical-student-organization-ctso.

Chapter 13

1 Colangelo, N. (2002). Counseling Gifted and Talented Students, The National Research Center on the Gifted and Talented (1990-2013). https://nrcgt.uconn.edu/newsletters/fall022/.

Chapter 14

1 Peters, S. J., Gentry, M., Whiting, G. W., & McBee, M. T. (2019). Who Gets Served in Gifted Education? Demographic Representation and a Call for Action. *Gifted Child Quarterly, 63*(4), 273–287.

PART THREE

Chapter 16

1 Montoya, R. M., Horton, R. S., & Kirchner, J. (2008). Is actual similarity necessary for attraction? A meta-analysis of actual and perceived similarity. *Journal of Social and Personal Relationships, 25*(6), 889–922. https://doi.org/10.1177/0265407508096700.

2 NAGC, Underachievement, https://www.nagc.org/resources-publications/resources/achievement-keeping-your-child-challenged/underachievement.

3 Adapted from NAGC.org, https://www.nagc.org/resources-publications/resources/achievement-keeping-your-child-challenged/underachievement.

Chapter 17

1 Collins, K. H., Price, E. F., Hanson, L., & Neaves, D. (2020). Consequences of Stereotype Threat and Imposter Syndrome: The Personal Journey from STEM-Practitioner to STEM-educator for Four Women of Color. Taboo: The Journal of Culture and Education, 19 (4). Retrieved from https://digitalscholarship.unlv.edu/taboo/vol19/iss4/10.

2 Hamacheck, D. E. (1978). Psychodynamics of normal and neurotic perfectionism. Psychology, 15, 27 – 33.

3 Yermish, A. (2012). Tips for Parents: Executive Functioning at Home and School, Davidson Institute for Talent Development, https://www.davidsongifted.org/search-database/entry/a10523.

Chapter 18

1 Klebold, S. (2016). ABC News, Diane Sawyer interview with Sue Klebold, https://abcnews.go.com/US/fullpage/diane-sawyer-exclusive-sue-klebold-36867525.

2 Siegle, D. (2013). The underachieving gifted child: Recognizing, understanding, and reversing underachievement. Waco, TX: Prufrock Press.

Chapter 19

1 Koplewicz, H., (2020). Being an Effective Advocate for Your Child. Child Mind Institute, https://childmind.org/article/being-an-effective-advocate-for-your-child/.

2 Kulik and Kulik, 1984B, Effects of Ability Grouping on Elementary School Pupils: A Meta-Analysis, Paper presented at the Annual Meeting of the American Psychological Association, 1984: https://eric.ed.gov/?id=ED255329.

3 Vialle, W, 2001, Acceleration: A coat of many colours, Roeper Review, V24.1: https://www.davidsongifted.org/search-database/entry/a10179.

4 Whitney, S. (2020). Parent Teacher Conference Checklist, Sign Up Genius, https://www.signupgenius.com/school/conference-checklist.cfm.

About the Author

Dr. Brenda Kay Small has served as an educator for over 20 years.

As an International Baccalaureate high school principal and middle school principal she learned how to effectively serve the needs of gifted students and their parents. Her education leadership strengths and advocacy for Gifted Education has led to multiple conference presentations, professional development for school leaders and teachers, publications, and consulting.

She earned the Administrator of the Year Award for her work in building schoolwide career academies that focus on preparing all levels of students for post-secondary success. As a Ford Next Generation Learning Community Coach, she works in communities nationwide to build partnerships between schools, businesses and universities.

Dr. Small loves to teach. Throughout her career, she has taught masters and doctoral level education leadership courses at four different universities in two states. She enjoys the challenge of writing contemporary and meaningful graduate level education leadership course curriculum. Her school leadership experience reaches beyond schools and into communities through the mentoring of future and new school leaders. As a classroom teacher, she received the Florida Social Science Teacher of the Year Award and the Florida's Excellence in Teaching Award.

Her primary research and professional interests are in education leadership relating to building strong student-centered schools. Her favorite quote comes from her father: "You get what you work for." The philosophy of hard work brings outstanding results for all.

She earned her doctorate and master's degrees from the University of South Florida in Education Leadership and Policy Studies. A true westerner, Dr. Small and her family enjoy living in her home state of Colorful Colorado.

Continue Your Quest to Advocate for Advanced Learners as a School Leader or Parent

Keep up with the latest publications, discussions and information on advocating for our high achievers. Together we can build communities of support for one of our nation's greatest natural resources: our children!!

Dr. Brenda Small is available to consult with your school or entity. Please contact her through her website at

www.leadsmarteducation.com

- ✔ Guest speaker availability for schools, districts, universities, conferences, companies, etc. Dr. Small will present a dynamic, entertaining, encouraging and information-filled presentation designed to meet your company's goals.
- ✔ Virtual book club meeting via ZOOM or SKYPE for school leaders, staff, parents, school counselors, policy makers, community advocates, etc.
- ✔ Stay in communication on social media. Join the chats on Facebook and Twitter to stay informed and add to the conversation on how to support our students of all learning levels, ideas for parents, school leadership discussions, etc.
- ✔ Visit the website for relevant publications supporting student-centered leadership.
- ✔ Watch the latest videos of Dr. Small's work, talks, media appearances and conference presentations as she discusses student-centered school leadership, parenting gifted students and advocacy for all levels of student learners.

CPSIA information can be obtained
at www.ICGtesting.com
Printed in the USA
FSHW010918100222
88210FS

9 781953 360052